TWAYNE'S WORLD AUTHORS SERIES
A Survey of the World's Literature

SPAIN

Janet W. Diaz, Texas Tech University

EDITOR

José López Rubio

TWAS 553

JOSÉ LÓPEZ RUBIO

By Marion Peter Holt

The College of Staten Island,
City University of New York

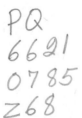
TWAYNE PUBLISHERS

A DIVISION OF G. K. HALL & CO., BOSTON

Copyright © 1980 by G.K. Hall & Co.

Published in 1980 by Twayne Publishers,
A Division of G.K. Hall & Co.
All Rights Reserved

Printed on permanent/ durable acid-free paper and bound
in the United States of America

First Printing

Frontispiece photograph of José López Rubio beside the Escorial.

Library of Congress Cataloging in Publication Data

Holt, Marion P
José López Rubio.

(Twayne's world authors series; TWAS 553: Spain)
Bibliography: p. 145-49
Includes index.
1. López Rubio, José—Criticism and interpretation.
PQ6621.O785Z68   862'.6'2   79-9784
ISBN 0-8057-6395-3

Contents

About the Author

Marion Peter Holt is on the faculty of the College of Staten Island of the City University of New York. He holds a Ph.D. degree from the University of Illinois and has taught courses in Spanish language and literature and in comparative literature at Queens College (CUNY) and at the University of Missouri –St. Louis. He is the author of *The Contemporary Spanish Theater, 1949–1972* and the editor of *The Modern Spanish Stage: Four Plays* and college text editions of dramatic works by José López Rubio and Víctor Ruiz Iriarte. He has directed productions in the United States of Buero Vallejo's *In the Burning Darkness* and *The Concert at Saint Ovide* and has translated plays by López Rubio, Casona, and Buero Vallejo.

Preface

José López Rubio has been a participant in virtually every aspect of the evolving performing arts of his time, and can be considered a "man of the theater" in the fullest sense. His theatrical experiences began in childhood, when his father took him to see the famed actors and actresses of the Benaventian period of Spanish drama. Later, he became a close associate of the other aspiring young playwrights of the 1920s—Jardiel Poncela, Neville, Mihura, Casona, and García Lorca—and attended the *tertulias* of the influential Gómez de la Serna. When he was only twenty-six, he came to the attention of the Madrid theater public with the premiere of *De la noche a la mañana* (Overnight), a play he had written in collaboration with Eduardo Ugarte. As a scenarist and adaptor of American films for Spanish productions in Hollywood in the 1930s, he provided the screenplays for almost all of the Martínez Sierra plays that were filmed in the United States. He enjoyed a warm and enduring friendship with Charles Chaplin, as well as rewarding contacts with many of the most creative artists of Hollywood's early years. His first assignment as a motion-picture director in his homeland was terminated by the outbreak of the Spanish Civil War. In 1949 he returned to the field that had always interested him most—the theater—and established himself as one of the most popular and respected contemporary Spanish dramatists.

López Rubio's creative endeavors have been varied and include a fine early novel, eighteen original full-length plays, two imaginative series of plays for television, and translations and adaptations of more than a score of foreign plays and musicals for the Spanish stage. He has been praised as a master of dialogue and, at the same time, accused of cultivating a theater of fantasy, of indulging in escapist comedy and avoiding the actualities of the contemporary world. Distracted by the surface brilliance and humor of many of his plays, some observers have failed to perceive the serious implications that underlie the subtle dialogue and the dramatic situations of his more important works. Like Anouilh in France, he has been particularly attracted by the role that illusion plays in human behavior, and the theatricalization of life by the characters themselves is a recurring device in both his serious comedies and in his lighter efforts. And, in much of his work, there is an unmistakable concern for the moral ambivalence of modern man and the changing moral and social perspectives in the second half of the twentieth century.

Like most other Spanish dramatists of the post–Civil War period, López Rubio has received only limited critical attention in the English-speaking world, and his plays have rarely been considered in depth. I have attempted in this first comprehensive treatment of his life and literary career to provide a clear understanding of his aesthetic and professional aims, the dramatic techniques that he has employed, and his special thematic interests. I have also attempted to identify his most important contributions and to define the qualities that give these works their special theatrical and literary value. At all times I have approached the plays—which constitute the major part of López Rubio's writing—as works that were created *for the theater* and to evaluate them in terms of their validity *in the theater*.

Since only one of López Rubio's plays has been published to date in English, descriptions of plot development and careful consideration of the dramatic treatment of key scenes are provided for all his more important plays, and somewhat briefer descriptions for his lesser dramatic works. Appropriate examples of dialogue are included in some instances to illustrate the style and content of a particular scene or play. Similar attention is given to the novel and to the collection of short stories published early in the writer's career. The translations of all passages of dialogue and of quotations from reviews and books which were originally written in Spanish are my own. The analyses of the plays from *Overnight* (*De la noche a la mañana*) to *Diana's Mind Is Busy* (*Diana está comunicando*) are essentially based on those made in my doctoral dissertation, *The Theatre of José López Rubio*, completed in 1964 at the University of Illinois under the direction of Professor William H. Shoemaker; and the detailed critiques of *Our Hands Are Innocent* (*Las manos son inocentes*) and *Alberto* are drawn in great part from articles published by me in *Hispania* (December 1966) and *Modern Drama* (September 1967), respectively. Biographical material has been obtained from some half-dozen interviews published by Spanish journalists and critics from 1951 to 1977, and from personal conversations with the playwright since 1965, particularly during the period September 8–October 4, 1977, in Madrid and El Escorial. For the chronology of the writer's life and career, I have relied in great part on the one provided by López Rubio himself for *Teatro selecto de José López Rubio*, published by Escelicer in 1969. Critical observations of every persuasion have been taken into consideration in the preparation of this study, but the final judgments in all instances are my own.

I am grateful to the playwright for making available to me the manuscripts of the unpublished *Cuenta nueva* (A New Account) and *La puerta del ángel* (The Way of the Angel), copies of the rare *Cuentos inverosímiles* (Unlikely Tales) and *Roque Six*, and the manuscripts of the fourteen episodes of the television series *Mujeres insólitas* (Exceptional Women) which had been completed at the time of writing. Also, I wish to acknowledge my indebtedness to William H. Shoemaker, who was instrumental in the decision to undertake my original study of the plays of López Rubio and who provided considered and understanding criticism during the preparation of that study. And I express special appreciation to Richard Medoff for his suggestions and invaluable assistance in the completion of the present book.

MARION PETER HOLT

New York, N.Y.

Chronology

1903   José López Rubio is born in Motril (Granada), Spain (December 13).

1904   His family moves to the city of Granada.

1909–   Granada: Attends a private school run by French nuns, sees
1914   his first theatrical performances, and performs in school functions.

1915–   Family resides in Madrid, and López Rubio attends the
1917   Colegio de los Agustinos. He attempts his first literary compositions, performs in school plays, and spends the summers in Galicia.

1917   Cuenca: Completes the *bachillerato* and writes a short play as part of "El día de Cuenca" celebration.

1919–   Madrid: Takes preparatory courses in law and begins his
1922   studies at the Universidad Central; enjoys his first literary friendships and attends the *tertulia* at the Café de Platerías; immersed in theater.

1922–   First articles and stories published in Madrid magazines and
1926   newspapers. Becomes an editor of *Buen humor* and attempts to write plays; completes his military service in the Cuartel de Artillería in Vicálvaro; collaborates with Jardiel Poncela on two plays which are never performed. Frequents the *tertulias* of Ramón Gómez de la Serna.

1924   Publication of *Cuentos inverosímiles*.

1926–   Collaborates with Edgar Neville on two comedies.
1928

1928–   Acts in the theater group *El Mirlo Blanco* in the home of the
1929   Barojas. Publication of the novel *Roque Six*. *De la noche a la mañana*, written with Eduardo Ugarte, wins the *A B C* contest for new playwrights and opens at the Reina Victoria theater on January 17, 1929.

1930   Premiere of *La casa de naipes*, also written with Ugarte. López Rubio receives a contract from Metro-Goldwyn-Mayer and departs for the United States.

1931   Receives a new contract to write screenplays for Fox Films and returns briefly to Spain.

1932–   Hollywood: Writes numerous screenplays and the first half of
1935   *Celos del aire*.

1936   Returns to Spain; writes screenplay for Benavente's *La malquerida*; production of film terminated by the outbreak of the Spanish Civil War on July 18. López Rubio leaves his homeland for France.

1937–   Returns to the United States and is given a new contract with
1938   20th-Century–Fox.

1938–   Mexico: Writes screenplays and translates; publishes the
1939   prose poem *Son triste*; travels to Cuba and New York City.

1940–   Returns to Spain and is involved in various aspects of film
1949   production; begins to write again for the stage.

1949   Premiere of *Alberto* on April 29, marking the beginning of López Rubio's second career as a playwright.

1950   Premiere of *Celos del aire* and the performance of the one-act play *Estoy pensando en ti*.

1951   *Veinte y cuarenta*, *Una madeja de lana azul celeste*, and *Cena de Navidad* performed. Awarded Fastenrath Prize of the Royal Spanish Academy for *Celos del aire*.

1952   Premiere of *El remedio en la memoria*.

1954   Productions of *La venda en los ojos*, *Cuenta nueva*, and *La otra orilla*.

1955   López Rubio receives National Prize for Theater for *La venda en los ojos*; also awarded the Alvarez Quintero Prize and the María Rolland Prize for Drama. Premiere of *El caballero de Barajas*, a musical comedy with score by Manuel Parada.

1956   Productions of *Un trono para Cristy* and *La novia del espacio*.

1958   Premiere of *Las manos son inocentes*, López Rubio's first play of tragic dimensions.

1960   A return to comedy: *Diana está comunicando*.

1961   Premiere of *Esta noche, tampoco*.

1963   Trips to Scandanavia and Brazil; works on screenplays and translations.

1964   Premiere of *Nunca es tarde*.

1965   Travels in South America.

1967   Fourth trip to the United States; gives seminars in several American colleges and universities.

1968–   El Escorial: Writes the drama *La puerta del ángel* and the
1969   television series *Al filo de lo imposible*.

Chronology

1971   Premiere of *Veneno activo* (adapted from television play of the same name).

1972   Production of *El corazón en la mano*; awarded the National Prize for Drama and the *El Alcázar* Prize.

1976   Telecast of *La segunda señora Tudor*, first of the series of television dramas *Mujeres insólitas*.

CHAPTER 1

Life and Career of a Man of the Theater

I The Early Years

A S a playwright of stage and television, a novelist, a film scenarist and director, and a translator, José López Rubio has lived in or close to centers of creative activity. But he began life in the small Mediterranean city of Motril, in southern Spain, where his father was temporarily in charge of family sugar-cane interests. The sixth and youngest child of Joaquín López Atienza and Magdalena Rubio Díaz, he was christened in Motril's Church of the Incarnation a few days after Christmas 1903 and formally assigned an array of Christian names that seems rather excessive for the man who would come to be known to his friends and close associates, inside and outside the theater, simply as "Pepe." [1]

López Rubio has described his father as a man who was liberal, inclined to politics, and addicted to the theater; and his mother as a devout woman who was at the same time very elegant and sophisticated. [2] In 1904 the family moved to Granada to a comfortable house with a carved facade on the Calle de Santa Teresa, and Joaquín López Atienza was able to pursue his interest in the theater in the relatively large provincial capital. He had a subscription to the municipal theater, was an inveterate "first-nighter," and cultivated people who were connected with the art that held so much fascination for him. As a child, López Rubio frequently accompanied his parents to performances by touring companies. On one occasion, he attended a rehearsal of Francisco Vallaespesa's *El alcázar de las perlas* (The Palace of the Pearls), which was being directed by Fernando Díaz de Mendoza, husband of the celebrated actress María Guerrero. It was the first time he had seen a theater from the stage, and the experience left a deep and lasting impression. [3]

From 1909 until 1914, López Rubio attended a private school run by French nuns in Granada. As soon as he was able to read, he discovered the *cartelera* (theater listings) in the newspaper *A B C*, and he eagerly participated in student theatricals sponsored by his school. Summers were spent quietly near the sea in Almería. In 1915 the family moved to Madrid, and José was enrolled in the Colegio of the Augustinians on the Calle Valverde, near their new residence. The young boy continued to attend the theater, to act in school plays, and to learn much about his father's second great passion: bullfighting. On the stage he saw María Guerrero, Carmen Cobeña, Emilio Thuillier, José Tallavi, and Rosario Pino; and, in the bullring, Antonio de Bilbao, Rafael el Gallo, Joselito, Belmonte, and other leading *toreros* of the period.

He completed his *bachillerato* in Cuenca after his father's appointment to the post of civil governor in that city. And it was in Cuenca that he wrote his first work for the stage—a one-act *sainete* in three scenes which was performed by a children's company, with music composed by the director of the municipal band. By the time he was sixteen, López Rubio had had the pleasure of seeing his first articles published in the local newspaper, *El día de Cuenca*. In 1919 he returned to Madrid to enroll in courses in law at the Universidad Central, but he was not long in abandoning his university studies to begin in earnest a career as a writer.

II *Madrid in the 1920s*

Madrid was a city of considerable intellectual and artistic activity in the 1920s. Most of the young men who were to become the leaders in peninsular writing in the mid-twentieth century resided in Spain's capital at one time or another during the decade. In the literary *tertulias* they came to know each other and, in many cases, developed friendships that were close and lifelong. New magazines and reviews were established to provide outlets for both writers and artists, and groups of aficionados organized to read and perform experimental plays that could not obtain commercial productions. If the city did not compare with Paris as a Mecca of the arts, it nevertheless provided opportunities, contacts, and an ambience that was favorable to the development of creative talents.

The commercial theater was dominated by Benavente, Arniches, the Quintero brothers, and playwrights of lesser renown such as Antonio Paso and García Alvarez; but Gregorio Martínez Sierra was soon to establish his influential theatrical company at the Teatro Eslava, off the Puerta del Sol, to produce not only the works of his wife and himself but also important modern and classic plays from the rest of Europe. And at the same time, he introduced new ideas of staging and production to the tradition-bound Spanish stage. It was Martínez Sierra who first recognized the promise of Federico García Lorca and staged his early play *El maleficio de la mariposa* (The Spell of the Butterfly) in 1920.

One of the most unusual literary personalities of the day—and one who held a particular fascination for young writers—was Ramón Gómez de la Serna. The *tertulias* he presided over at the Café Pombo, in the Calle Carretas, were the most famous intellectual gatherings in the capital and attracted not only the new generation of creative young men in Madrid but also literary figures from Europe and Latin America. Gómez de la Serna's own attempts at theater were not commercially viable, but his plays and other writings held great appeal for those who were seeking to break away from the prevailing conventions. His bohemian air and new and frequently startling way with language made him irresistible.

Soon after his return to Madrid in 1919, José López Rubio's name became familiar to the reading public as his stories and articles began to appear in *Nuevo Mundo, La Nación, La Esfera, Los Lunes de El Imparcial, Blanco y Negro*, and *El Sol*. His talent was quickly recognized, and he took an active part in the operations of *Buen Humor*, an important and influential humor magazine founded by Pedro Antonio Villahermosa. He frequented several literary *tertulias*, including the Platerías and the Sagrada Cripta de Pombo of Gómez de la Serna, and became a close associate of Enrique Jardiel Poncela, Edgar Neville, Tono, and other figures of the theater, art, and journalism.

The first book by López Rubio, a collection of short stories called *Cuentos inverosímiles* (Unlikely Tales), was published in 1924, when the author was not yet twenty-one years old. Each story was preceded with an illustration—most by artists and cartoonists (such as Sileno, K-Hito, and Tono) who were already well known or on the threshold of recognition. Some of the stories were little more than sketches, but all were written with a sense of style and clearly demonstrated the young author's imagination and inventiveness.

In spite of his decided talent for prose and journalism, López Rubio remained strongly attracted to the theater. During this period he was attempting to write plays in collaboration with Enrique Jardiel Poncela, who was three years his senior and who had already enjoyed some modest recognition as a playwright. By 1924 they had completed *Un hombre de bien* (A Reputable Man) and presented it to the management of the Teatro Lara for consideration; however, the work was not performed, and a second play attempted by the two writers, *El anõ 2.550* (The Year 2550), was never completed. López Rubio was also collaborating with Edgar Neville. Together they wrote two comedies: *Al fin sola* (Alone at Last) and *Luz a las ánimas*.[4] The first of these was actually performed in 1928, but only after it had been rewritten and adapted by the successful playwright Honorio Maura, who changed the title to *Su mano derecha* (His Right Hand). In its final form it was a light comedy of romantic intrigue, with a contemporary setting and a rather improbable plot.[5] López Rubio and Neville received some royalties from the production, but their names were not directly associated with the play.

In 1928 López Rubio published *Roque Six*, an episodic novel in which the antihero appears in six incarnations and must endure a death for each life until the cycle is finally broken. It was a fine achievement, touched with dark humor and containing elements of potent antimilitaristic satire in one episode that might well have prevented the novel's publication had it been completed in the post–Civil War period. The same year, the Madrid daily *A B C* sponsored a playwriting contest for new authors, assuring the winning play a professional production. López Rubio submitted two works: *Luz a las ánimas*, which he had written with Neville, and *De la noche a la mañana* (Overnight), a serious comedy written in collaboration with Eduardo Ugarte Pagés. There were 884 entries in the competition—testimony to the creative activity in Spain on the eve of the Republic—and the prize was awarded to *Overnight*, with the premiere taking place on January 17, 1929, in the Teatro Reina Victoria. The play was a critical and popular success, and adaptations were made for productions in Portugal, Italy, and England. The reviewer for *La Esfera*, in a somewhat flowery style, praised the work for its originality and avoidance of theatrical clichés and noted the quality of the authors' style: "They employ language for its proper function, not for juggling acts with words. . . . They speak with simplicity: divine simplicity! Only artists capable of realizing their concepts with it [simplicity] truly reach the spectator, and by this route, immortality."[6] López Rubio was satisfied that he had proven himself in the field that interested him most; and now that he could expect some real financial gain from his writing, he went off on his first trip to Paris.

On May 27, 1930, a second play by López Rubio and Ugarte—quite different in tone from their first—was performed in the Teatro

Español. *La casa de naipes* (The House of Cards), a realistic drama about destroyed illusions, was also well received by the critics, although there were some reservations about the final act, which seemed too long and verbose. Evidently the young playwrights took due note of the critical comments, for *A B C* reported a few days after the premiere that some cuts had been made in the third act, increasing its effectiveness.

The third effort of the two authors, *Mitad y mitad* (Half and Half), did not reach the production stage. Dealing with a man who believes that he has found his dead wife in the form of two women, the comedy was rejected as being "too daring." The actress Irene López Heredia then requested a new play from López Rubio and Ugarte. The work, a comedy about a bank failure, was to have been entitled *Crac*, but the writing was never completed. The director of the Alba-Bonafé company, who had been one of the judges for the *A B C* contest in which *Overnight* had been selected, expressed an interest in producing the López Rubio–Neville play *Luz a las ánimas*, but this project also failed to materialize. If these minor setbacks caused disappointment, it was quickly assuaged by the offer of a contract to write dialogue for Spanish versions of American films produced at Metro-Goldwyn-Mayer studios in Hollywood; and, in August of 1930, López Rubio abandoned his theatrical activities in Madrid and sailed for the United States.

III   *The Hollywood Years*

In 1928 and 1929, the advent of talking pictures revolutionized the motion-picture industry. No longer could the large Hollywood studios accommodate their foreign markets simply by supplying titles for their films in the appropriate language as had been the practice in the silent era. Although dubbing was already possible (and RKO had begun by dubbing *Rio Rita* into Spanish in 1929), this technique was not to become popular for a number of years.[7] Metro, Paramount, Fox, and other studios decided to produce foreign versions of some of their films—frequently shot simultaneously with the English-language version and utilizing the same sets—with foreign artists assuming the roles of their American counterparts. Since the Spanish-speaking countries represented the largest foreign market for the new talking pictures, special departments were set up to supply the demand. Not only did the companies need actors and actresses who could perform in Spanish, they also had to have words for them to speak.

López Rubio's contract to prepare Spanish versions of English-language scripts for Metro had been arranged by Edgar Neville, who had lived in the United States as a diplomatic attaché and had already begun to work in the motion-picture capital; and it was Neville who met the young writer at the station in Los Angeles. López Rubio barely had time to drop his luggage at his hotel before being whisked off to a swimming pool where, on his first day in Hollywood, he met Charlie Chaplin (known in Spain as "Charlot"), whose friendship he was to value above that of all others during the Hollywood years. López Rubio dined frequently with Chaplin and became a regular at the social functions at the famous comedian's home. Chaplin would entertain with devastating imitations of other prominent figures of the motion-picture world, or one of his guests would perform (Albert Einstein obliged with his violin). There were also screenings of important avant-garde films, and it was at Chaplin's that López Rubio first saw Eisenstein's *Battleship Potemkin* and Buñuel's *Le Chien Andalou*.

As his command of spoken English improved, López Rubio had no difficulty in making friends in California, especially among the actors, actresses, and directors at MGM. Unlike Jardiel Poncela, who was also under contract at the same studio and dissatisfied with the milieu, López Rubio thoroughly appreciated the advantages of working steadily and creatively for a good salary, while enjoying the company of some of the most stimulating people then living in Hollywood. The gatherings at Chaplin's might seem a far cry from the Saturday-night *tertulias* in Madrid at the "Sacred Crypt" of Pombo, but in some ways they must have been similar.

Eduardo Ugarte was also under contract with Metro, and the authors of *Overnight* and *The House of Cards* collaborated on the Spanish versions of *Madame X* (*La mujer X*), *The Trial of Mary Dugan* (*El proceso de Mary Dugan*), and a talking version of the silent film *The Gay Deceiver* called *Su última noche*. When the studio decided to close its Spanish department in 1932, López Rubio moved to the Spanish division of Fox Films (later called 20th-Century–Fox). There he was to acquire a knowledge of all aspects of film-making and participate in the production of some fifteen Spanish-language motion pictures. As Carlos Fernández Cuenca has written, "The dozen most notable of these [films] . . . spoken in [Spanish] that came out of Hollywood studios between 1931 and 1935 carry the significant credit of the writer from Granada." [8] After a final collaboration with López Rubio on an original production called *Mi último amor* (My Last

Love), Eduardo Ugarte returned to Spain, and their literary association ended.

López Rubio's first solo adaptation was *Marido y mujer*, the Spanish version of Frank Borzage's *Bad Girl* (1932), but the several assignments that followed were adaptations of plays by the Martínez Sierras.[9] Gregorio Martínez Sierra had been named director of the Spanish division at Fox in 1931, and six of his works were filmed in Spanish between 1932 and 1935. All but one of the screen adaptations (*Mamá*, 1931), were prepared by José López Rubio. He also wrote the original script or the adaptation for six other films during the period, including *Rosa de Francia* (1935), the screen version of the play by Eduardo Marquina and L. Fernández Ardavin, and *El último varón sobre la tierra* (It's Great to be Alive, 1933), the single Spanish production that was filmed prior to an English version.

Although busily engaged in cinematic work, López Rubio had not lost interest in his career as a dramatist. In 1935 he began work on *Celos del aire* (In August We Play the Pyrenees),[10] the play that would establish him as a major playwright after its premiere in Madrid fifteen years later. He completed more than half of the first act in Hollywood before returning to Spain under contract to the producer Saturnino Ulargui to direct several motion pictures. The filming of his first production in Spain, a version of Benavente's *La malquerida* (known as *The Passion Flower* in the United States), was scheduled to begin on July 20, 1936, but was halted by the outbreak of the Spanish Civil War.

After the beginning of hostilities in Spain, López Rubio remained in Madrid for a short period, attempting to write in his room at the Hotel Savoy; then he left the country for France. He resumed the writing of *Celos del aire* and completed the first act before returning to the United States to work briefly for Fox once again. In 1939 he went to Mexico to prepare a scenario for a film version of Jorge Isaacs's novel *María*; however, the war in Spain ended, and López Rubio decided to go back to his homeland, leaving the script of *María* unfinished. During his stay in Mexico, he worked on the second act of *Celos del Aire* and also a new play that he had planned to call *La guerra se ha declarado esta tarde* (War Was Declared This Afternoon). When World War II swept over Europe in the final months of 1939, the playwright put aside the comedy with the ominous title. Having embarked from Cuba for New York at the end of December— the beginning of a long trip home—López Rubio welcomed in a new 1940 at sea.

IV   A Second Career in Spain

Although theatrical performances resumed in Madrid within days
after the fall of the capital to the Nationalist forces of General Franco
in 1939, there were few plays produced that could be considered
innovative or challenging for almost a decade following the end of the
Spanish Civil War. Censorship and economic stringencies had their
stifling effects on all forms of creativity. Only López Rubio's longtime
friend and associate Enrique Jardiel Poncela succeeded in staging
works that offered a degree of originality and, in their special way,
intellectual interest. But it was that specialist in escapist, ephemeral
comedy, Conrado Torrado, who brought the most patrons into the
theaters.

In 1940 the filming of *La malquerida* was finally realized, and until
1947 López Rubio devoted himself principally to scriptwriting and
directing films. He was associated with the productions of *Pepe
Conde, Rosa de Africa, Luna de Sangre, La petenera*, and *A la lima y
al limón* in 1941; *Sucedió en Damasco* in 1942; *Eugenia de Montijo* in
1944; *El crimen de Pepe Conde* in 1946; and, finally, *Alhucemas* in
1947. For a year and a half after the filming of *Eugenia de Montijo*
López Rubio was not engaged in motion-picture work. He found time
to write for the stage again, and it was during this period that he
completed both *Alberto* (originally called *Alfredo*) and *Una madeja de
lana azul celeste* (A Skein of Sky-Blue Wool). In 1947 his adaptation of
Benn W. Levy's *Mrs. Moonlight* (*El tiempo dormido*) was performed
in Madrid and, the following year, his new version of Molière's classic
comedy *Le bourgeois gentilhomme* (*El burgués gentilhombre*). Late
in 1948, he read the first act of *Celos del aire* to the prominent actor
Guillermo Marín, who brought the play to the attention of the
director Cayetano Luca de Tena. It was requested for performance
during the next season at the Teatro Español. The author then read
both *Alberto*, a complex serious comedy with an imaginary protagonist, and *A Skein of Sky-Blue Wool*, a lighter comedy of domestic
intrigue, to Luis Escobar, who selected the more challenging work
and directed its production at the Teatro María Guerrero in 1949.

The premiere of *Alberto*, on April 29, 1949, marked the beginning
of López Rubio's second career as a playwright and the start of his
most important period of creative activity. Although the two collaborative plays with Ugarte had brought him a degree of recognition, he
had chosen a firm contract in Hollywood over the less certain oppor-

tunities in the Madrid theater. Now, for the first time, an independently written work of his was staged. *Alberto* did not receive the critical acclaim that some of López Rubio's subsequent plays inspired, but it was a work of genuine artistic merit and a clear reaffirmation of the author's talent.

Celos del aire, which had been written before *Alberto*, opened less than a year later, on January 25, 1950. It elicited admiring praise from both critics and audiences and confirmed López Rubio's position in the contemporary Spanish theater. Alfredo Marquerie was prompted to declare that this intellectual comedy was "one of the best constructed and intelligent . . . theatrical pieces of our time." [11] The play won the Fastenrath Prize of the Royal Spanish Academy and, after its presentation in Buenos Aires, the Rosario de Santa Fe Prize for the best foreign production of the year. In 1951 it was performed in Italy under the title *Due più due, sei* (Two Plus Two Are Six). Even in Mexico, where critics were not notably receptive to new dramatic works from the mother country, Julio Sapietsa wrote in *El Universal*: ". . . This play is constructed point by point, developed with a great understanding of all aspects of the theater; and, nevertheless, it is also life with the emotions of life, although expressed in a different form, with humor. . . ." [12] At the end of the 1949–50 season, a minor short play, *Estoy pensando en ti* (I'm Thinking of You), written by López Rubio especially for an evening of tributes to Guillermo Marín, was performed in the Teatro Español.

The performances of López Rubio's two intellectual comedies of quality came at a time when Spain's stagnant theater was entering a period of revitalization—signaled most notably by the productions of *Historia de una escalera* (Story of a Stairway) and *En la ardiente oscuridad* (In The Burning Darkness), by Antonio Buero Vallejo, winner of the Lope de Vega Prize for 1949. Buero's first play was hailed by critics as a turning point in Spanish drama, and he quickly became the most discussed new playwright of the post–Civil War period. And Alfonso Sastre was preparing to bring controversy to the theatrical scene with his plays of even stronger social and political implications and to speak out boldly against the restrictions of censorship. López Rubio was not the only writer of the prewar generation to make a positive contribution during this period of theatrical renovation. Miguel Mihura's *Tres sombreros de copa* (Three Top Hats) was finally staged in 1952 (after a wait of some two decades), and this outstanding humorist also began to devote himself exclusively to the theater. Edgar Neville became active again and wrote *El Baile* (The

Dance), the most successful sentimental comedy of the decade. This bittersweet work contained no social message and was attacked as an example of *teatro de evasión*, but on its own terms it was an excellent piece of theater.

The career of Joaquín Calvo-Sotelo, a contemporary of López Rubio and Mihura, reached its peak in 1954 with *La muralla* (The Wall), the first drama to deal with events of the Spanish Civil War in any meaningful way. Víctor Ruiz Iriarte, a somewhat younger playwright, was beginning to show an unmistakable style and aesthetic point of view with *El landó de seis caballos* (The Six-Horse Landau, 1950), *Juego de niños* (A Dangerous Game, 1952), and *El pobrecito embustero* (The Poor Deceiver, 1953). If most of the plays seen in Madrid in the 1950s were stronger on poetics than on political statements or social criticism, they were nevertheless equal in artistic merit to (and in certain instances superior to) most of the dramatic works produced in Europe and America during the period. If Spain did not have an Ionesco or Beckett who exerted an influence beyond a single theatrical center, neither did the United States or England.

V   *The Course of the Second Career*

Firmly established by the success of *Celos del aire*, López Rubio had three new plays performed in less than a year: *Veinte y cuarenta* (Twenty and Forty), February 8, 1951; *Cena de Navidad* (Christmas Dinner), November 14, 1951; and *Una madeja de lana azul celeste* (A Skein of Sky-Blue Wool), December 7, 1951. But none of these works was able to equal the popular or critical success of the earlier play. In a survey of the theatrical offerings of the year written for *Indice*, García-Luengo devoted only brief mention and faint praise to López Rubio's contributions: "He glories in a dialogue stitched together with clever thoughts, although of meager theatrical inventiveness." [13] *Christmas Dinner*, which was serious in tone, was the least popular of the new plays—and perhaps the best. Sainz de Robles, in his observations on the 1951 season, expressed his admiration for the first act of the work: " . . . for my taste, the first act of *Christmas Dinner*, with the first act of *Alberto*, are the finest accomplishments . . . of López Rubio. It would be difficult to conceive anything finer in technical mastery, wit, human interest, and poetry." [14] Whatever the flaws and merits of the play, it represented an attempt by the author to extend his dramatic range, and it marked the beginning of his close professional association with the talented actress Conchita Montes, who essayed the principal female role in the play and for whom the playwright would develop more important roles in the future.

For the 1952 season, López Rubio wrote one of his finer plays, *El remedio en la memoria* (Remedy in Memory), for another excellent actress, Tina Gascó, who created the leading role (though perhaps not as adequately as might have been expected). The Pirandellian affinity that the playwright had already demonstrated in *Alberto, Celos del aire*, and one memorable scene in *Christmas Dinner* was especially pronounced in this drama which dealt with the inability of an actress to separate her private life from the roles she has performed on stage. Torrente Ballester, who had expressed many reservations about the playwright's earlier works, found the new play worthy of acclaim and emphasized its literary values. [15] But López Rubio felt pique that not all the critics were as appreciative as Torrente of a play that he had written with particular dedication.

Fifteen months were to pass before his next play was offered to the public, but López Rubio was far from inactive. In addition to writing original works, he had been engaged in adapting foreign plays for the Spanish stage. Since 1947 he had received numerous commissions for adaptations, and the time-consuming work had provided good financial remuneration. One of the most discussed and admired productions of the 1952 season had been his translation of Arthur Miller's *Death of a Salesman* (*La muerte de un viajante*), and his adaptation of Oscar Wilde's *The Importance of Being Earnest* (*La importancia de llamarse Ernesto*) was performed successfully in both Madrid and Barcelona. The critic Enrique Sordo praised the language of the new version of the Wilde comedy, though he felt that the translator had not succeeded in capturing completely the play on words that gives the work its title (to be sure, an impossibility in Spanish). [16] Carlos Fernández Cuenca observed: "López Rubio is, without doubt, one of the few Spanish authors who could put the very brilliant dialogue of Wilde into our language—since his own customary dialogue is no less brilliant. In this case the translator has succeeded in carrying out the difficult task of bringing Spanish wit to the English text without deforming it in the least. . . ." [17] Other translations by the playwright in the early 1950s include Deval's *Tovarich*, 1950, and *Ombre Chère* (*Sombra querido*), 1952; Maugham's *The Constant Wife* (*La esposa constante*), 1952; Fodor's *Europa and the Bull* (*Europa y el toro*), 1953; and Knott's *Dial M for Murder* (*Crimen perfecto*), 1953.

With the production of *La venda en los ojos* (The Blindfold) in March of 1954, López Rubio added substantially to his reputation. The play dealt with the refusal of a young woman to accept the reality

of her husband's desertion and her creation of an illusory world with
two elderly allies. With its blend of absurdist humor, genuine human
conflicts, and poetic undercurrents, it proved to be the author's most
important undertaking since *Celos del aire*. Torrente Ballester found
it an admirable work: "It is, in my opinion, López Rubio's best
play. . . . It doesn't matter to me a whit whether it's *teatro de
evasión* or not, because it is theater and because all the elements of
the comedy, absolutely all, are handled with a skill, with assurance,
and with an efficacy that justify the escape, the evasion, or the flight
[from reality]. . . ." [18] Fernández Cuenca, in a review for *Teatro*,
echoed Torrente's opinions: "*The Blindfold* seems to us to be one of
the best contemporary Spanish comedies. . . . The psychological
probing that comes through from time to time in the torrent of wit and
humor, the wealth of subtle details that enhance both situations and
dialogue . . . are values that are present in abundance." [19]

But success does not necessarily follow success in the theater. The
premiere of López Rubio's next play, *Cuenta nueva* (A New
Account), took place in Barcelona, where it did not have a favorable
reception. One reviewer considered the work dated and unconvinc-
ing, the dialogue discursive and reminiscent of Benavente. [20] Julio
Coll, while not admiring the play, wrote somewhat more kindly of the
production and even found in it moments of excellence. [21] *A New
Account* did not reach Madrid, but it is unlikely that it would have
been successful if it had been staged in the capital. The play simply
did not measure up to the standards the playwright had already set.

A few weeks after the Barcelona opening, López Rubio had occasion to forget, for the first performance of *La otra orilla* (The Other
Shore), on November 4, 1954, in the Teatro de la Comedia in Madrid,
was met with the kind of enthusiastic approval *The Blindfold* had
received. When the play opened in Barcelona a few months after its
Madrid premiere, the very critic who had disliked *A New Account* so
thoroughly expressed the opinion that López Rubio had now written
a fine play, superior to *Celos del aire*. [22] Without question it was a
critical point in López Rubio's second career, for, as the editors of the
subsequent textbook edition of the play have pointed out, comparison with the immensely successful *The Blindfold* was inevitable. [23]
The two plays were, of course, quite different in tone; but regardless
of how *The Other Shore* might compare with the earlier work under
close scrutiny, its merits were more than sufficient to rank it among
the playwright's best and most important plays.

The dramatic situation of *The Other Shore* reflected the interest in the fantastic and the supernatural that López Rubio had shown in *Overnight*, the unperformed *Half and Half*, his novel *Roque Six*, and some of the early short stories. The four principal characters are killed in the opening scene and, as ghosts, are able to consider for a while the lies and follies of their recent lives, revealed in sobering but hardly lugubrious detail. The illusion is skillfully established at the beginning and sustained through the poignant final moments of the play. *The Other Shore* had, of course, been preceded by many plays in which ghosts or spirits appear—of most recent memory Jardiel Poncela's *Un marido de ida y vuelta* (A Round Trip Husband, 1939) and Noel Coward's *Blithe Spirit* (1941).[24] López Rubio's ironic comedy bore only slight resemblance to these popular works. The essential and telling difference was that this play was developed from the point of view of the dead, whose plane of reality the audience joins, rather than that of the living. Furthermore, it provoked serious reflection on the moral condition of contemporary man while providing the intelligent humor and deft satire of the clichés and rituals of human communication for which the playwright was becoming famous.

López Rubio's next venture was the preparation of the book and lyrics for a musical comedy called *El caballero de Barajas* (The Gentleman from Barajas). Manuel Parada composed the music, the playwright himself directed the production, and the work was first performed on September 23, 1955, in the Teatro Alcázar. The musical had a contemporary setting, and the dialogue and songs were filled with topical allusions. Although it was only a pleasant entertainment with elements of satire, it was named the best musical production of the season. The same year, López Rubio's adaptation of Rodgers and Hammerstein's *South Pacific* (*Al sur del Pacífico*) opened to a good critical reception, though not the kind of public enthusiasm that the musical had inspired in the United States.

In February of 1956, the playwright presented another new play in Barcelona and met with the most unequivocal failure of his career. With its "flying saucer" theme, *La novia del espacio* (The Love from Space) might have been expected to have considerable appeal for the public. During the year prior to the premiere of the play, a Barcelona periodical had devoted considerable space to the speculations about the many reports of mysterious objects in the skies. But the critics were unimpressed, and their comments were uniformly negative.

The play was never staged in Madrid, and López Rubio's plans to revise the work were never carried out.

Un trono para Cristy (A Throne for Cristy), which opened in Madrid on September 14,1956, was a more typical comedy dealing with the efforts of an American woman living in Mallorca to achieve royal status for her daughter. With a strong cast headed by Isabel Garcés, Julia Gutiérrez Caba, and the character actress Irene Caba Alba, it proved a successful production, though some critics considered it a *pièce rose* that was not up to López Rubio's highest standards and ignored the satire of contemporary pretentions that he had attempted to inject into the play. In 1960 it was published in the United States, becoming the third work by the playwright to appear in a textbook edition.

In 1957, López Rubio made an adaptation of Lope de Vega's *La estrella de Sevilla* (The Star of Seville), which was staged with background music by F. Moraleda Bellver and Luis Moraleda Bellver. The following year, at the beginning of the fall theatrical season, the playwright offered a new original work, a serious drama which represented a total departure from humoristic theater and a new direction in his artistic development. In *Las manos son inocentes* (Our Hands Are Innocent) López Rubio had made no concessions to popular taste. Modern in tone but a tightly constructed play of classical lineage, the work dealt with the problem of guilt and the power of social deprivation to break down the moral constraints of a man and his wife and to lead them to attempt a bloodless murder. The critical commentaries were numerous and, for the most part, respectful, although not always characterized by depth of perception. Buero Vallejo, now the leader among the creators of serious drama in contemporary Spain, publicly expressed his admiration for the courage that López Rubio had shown in risking the possibilities of commercial failure and in venturing into new areas of dramatic expression.[25] But the admirers of the new play remained a minority, and the public did not rush to the theater in search of dramatic veracity.

Although the climate for serious drama in Spain was somewhat more favorable in the decade that followed the production of *Our Hands Are Innocent*, López Rubio did not elect to continue his experimentation. His next two plays were comedies, replete with humorous situations, the customary sparkling dialogue, and deft touches of satire. Both *Diana está comunicando* (Diana's Mind Is Busy), in 1960, and *Esta noche, tampoco* (Not Tonight, Either), in

1961, were designed for the talents of Conchita Montes; and the popular comedienne was well received in both plays. The former work was an exceptionally funny play—the closest to farce that López Rubio had written—about the amorous intrigues of a beautiful and witty mental telepathist; and the second was an excellent satirical comedy about the wife of an oil magnate and her frustrated suitors. Neither play had the poetic overtones of *The Blindfold* or *The Other Shore*, but both were well-crafted entertainments. And in *Not Tonight, Either* the playwright demonstrated once again that a Pirandellian technique could be utilized skillfully and unobtrusively for comic and satirical purposes.

In 1961 there were also productions of several of López Rubio's translations: William Gibson's *Two for the Seesaw* (*Dos en un balancín*) and *The Miracle Worker* (*El milagro de Ana Sullivan*), and *The Two Sebastians* (*Los dos Sebastiani*) of Howard Lindsay and Russell Crouse. These were followed in 1962 by Maxwell Anderson's *Joan of Lorraine* (*Juana de Lorena*) and Montherlant's *Le Cardinal d'Espagne* (*El cardenal de España*).

VI *A Change of Pace*

Now, after more than fifteen years of almost continual involvement in the theater—writing, translating, and participating in various aspects of production—López Rubio slowed his pace, and his name was no longer inevitably conspicuous in the theater listings as a new season got under way. Throughout his second career, he had periodically escaped from the commotion, the telephone calls, and the social commitments of Madrid to dedicate himself to his writing. Most of the final act of *Celos del aire* had been written in a country place called Zarzuela del Monte, on the very edge of the province of Madrid; *Twenty and Forty* was completed in El Paular; the second act of *Christmas Dinner* was written in the Canary Islands; and the composition of *Remedy in Memory* was begun in Tangiers and completed in San Lorenzo del Escorial. In the 1960s Madrid was growing rapidly, and with economic prosperity came air pollution and an influx of outsiders. López Rubio had found a retreat in a turn-of-the-century hotel in El Escorial, some forty miles from the capital and almost literally in the shadow of the vast edifice constructed by Felipe II in the sixteenth century. Here the air was clear and the nights serene, yet the lights of Madrid were still visible in the distance. López Rubio began to spend more and more of his time in these agreeable surroundings, while maintaining his apartment in the city. He also began to indulge one of his favorite pastimes: travel. In 1963 he took trips to Scandanavia and Brazil, and two years later he took another trip to South America, visiting Argentina and Brazil.

It was not until 1964 that López Rubio's next original play, *Nunca es tarde* (It's Never Too Late), was staged. The production boasted a strong cast headed by two of Spain's foremost performers, Enrique Diosdado and Amelia de la Torre, and featured the young actor Rafael Guerrero in the juvenile lead. *It's Never Too Late* contained polished and ingenious dialogue, poetic undercurrents, and a temporary flight from reality—all qualities associated with López Rubio's theater. But in spite of an optimistic ending, it was decidedly a *pièce noire* in which a principal character is tragically killed at the end of the second act.

The next hiatus in López Rubio's career, at least as far as original works for the stage were concerned, was much longer. However, he prepared a number of screenplays and completed translations of Norman Krasna's *Sunday in New York* (*Un Domingo en Nueva York*, 1964), Dale Wasserman's *Man of La Mancha* (*Hombre de la Mancha*, 1966), Rodgers and Hammerstein's *The Sound of Music* (*Sonrisas y lágrimas*, 1968), and Philippe Adrien's *La Baye* (*La baiiiiia*, 1968). In the winter of 1966–67, he was invited to be playwright-in-residence at Hiram College, in Ohio, and returned to the United States for the first time in twenty-eight years. After his stay in Ohio, he conducted seminars at the State University of New York in Albany and at the University of Missouri–St. Louis and then traveled on to California for a visit to the film capital that he had left some thirty years before, only to find it drastically changed from its heyday.

In the late 1960s, López Rubio completed *La puerta del ángel* (The Way of the Angel), a serious drama with frank sexual motivations that represented as much of a departure from his serious comedies as *Our Hands Are Innocent* had in 1958. Despite the dramatic strengths of this atypical work, no producer could be found who would risk a staging, and the play was put aside. At this point in his career, López Rubio found a new and productive outlet for his creative talents by turning to television drama. His series of short plays called *Al filo de lo imposible* (At the Edge of the Impossible) was telecast in 1970 and received both the Premio Ondas and the Premio Nacional for the best dramatic works written for television that year. The episodes of the series varied considerably in theme, mood, and development—from black or ironic comedies such as *La casi viuda* (Almost a Widow) to a Jardielesque romp with bungling kidnappers in two parts entitled *El secuestro* (The Kidnapping) and *El rescate* (The Ransoming). In a totally different vein there was also the outstanding *El último hilo* (The Last Connection), a memorable depiction of old age and destroyed illusions. One of the best of the series, *Veneno activo* (Active Poison), was adapted for the stage and opened at the Café Teatro Stefanis on October 21, 1971, to favorable reviews. It was a small but striking exercise in ironic, macabre theater in which the dialogue was intentionally deformed to resemble an overly literal translation into Spanish of a French play. Café theaters were at their peak of popularity in Madrid when *Active Poison* was staged, and the three-character play fitted well into the intimate surroundings.

Finally, the following year, a new full-length work was accepted for production. *El corazón en la mano* (With Heart in Hand) opened on March 23, 1972, at the Teatro Benavente, with Ismael Merlo in the leading role. *With Heart in Hand* dealt with a dual moral dilemma faced by a man who has the "problem" of being too decent, too honest, and too unselfish to further his own business and romantic interests. He makes a decision to take his share of worldly rewards rather than grow old as a failure, in loneliness and boredom. In structuring the play, López Rubio abandoned the three-act format of his earlier works in favor of a series of seven terse scenes which carry the protagonist from a kind of professional and emotional limbo to the point that he no longer is ruled by his heart. Although the play lacked the sheer theatricality of the writer's most memorable serious comedies, it commanded respect, and one major critic (Adolfo Prego) ranked it with *Celos del aire* and *The Other Shore*.[26] Later in the year it won for López Rubio the National Prize for Drama.

It was in the field of television drama that López Rubio's most interesting writing for the 1970s was achieved. His second series of television plays, entitled *Mujeres insólitas* (Exceptional Women), was undertaken after extensive research into the lives of some thirteen famous or near-famous women of history and the literary treatments and legends they have inspired. Some of his subjects, such as Cleopatra, Alfonsine Plessis (Camille), and Lola Montes, had an international fame; others, such as Juana la loca and Inés de Castro are less well known outside the Iberian Peninsula but have been the subjects of many literary treatments. López Rubio's hour-long dramas served to demythify his heroines and to allow them to present their own versions of the truth and their reactions to the literary liberties taken with their stories by writers of different periods and the distortions that exist in their legendary personae. Each of the plays begins on a bare set, with a stage manager and the central character present. Techniques of alienation and distancing are used liberally, and scenes from other versions of the women's lives are interpolated with remarkable dramatic effect.

López Rubio has worked intermittently on other writing projects. For almost two decades he has collected material for a history and encyclopedia of Spanish theater. He has also written critical introductions to books on several major figures of Spanish literature and occasional essays on theater and personalities of the stage and film with whom he has been associated. But his abiding passion has been theater—in the total sense of the word; and a deep commitment to this art has consistently directed the application of his creative energies.

CHAPTER 2

The First Literary Period

I   Cuentos inverosímiles (*Unlikely Tales*)

THE young López Rubio was quickly drawn into the literary and artistic life of Madrid when he returned to the capital at the age of nineteen to continue his academic studies. Through his contributions to literary journals and magazines and his attendance at the most important literary gatherings, his talent was recognized and encouraged. His first book, a collection of short stories and sketches entitled *Cuentos inverosímiles* (Unlikely Tales), was published in 1924, when the author was not yet twenty-one years old. Considerable care was given to the makeup of the book, and each of the "tales" was illustrated by a prominent or an aspiring artist of the period—among them K-Hito, Sileno, Bagaria, Sirio, Tono, and the author's own brother Paco.[1] The twenty-one stories, some of them little more than brief, whimsical sketches, vary in length, quality, and interest. But a sure sense of style and a feeling for the felicitous descriptive phrase are evident throughout the collection. The best and longest of the stories, "La tía Germana" (Aunt Germana), is an unforgettable study of evolving or feigned madness as seen through the eyes of a young boy.

The variety of subject matter in the collection clearly demonstrates López Rubio's remarkable inventiveness and range. However, not all of his situations are developed satisfactorily, and some of the briefer tales are terminated by a twist or an attempt at irony that seems forced and artificial. For example, in "El Record" (The Record) a group of athletes boasting of their accomplishments in an elegant bar are called to task by an old man who has been sipping his coffee and listening from a nearby table. He tells them that he is not impressed. When they inquire as to his reasons, he informs them that he is accustomed to greater distances, and reveals that he is Ahasvero, The Wandering Jew. The opening anecdote, "El corsario" (The Corsaire), records the mishaps of an African lion destined for a zoo who takes over the operations of the Italian liner that is transporting him to

Hamburg. The events are whimsical, ironic, and truly unlikely. Another story, "El tributo de las cien plumas" (The Tribute of the Hundred Feathers), also attributes powers to a creature that does not in reality possess them—in this case a bird of paradise who bargains with a hunter about to shoot him for his plumage. Both "El espíritu de Arsenio Lupin" (The Spirit of Arsene Lupin) and "La consulta" (The Consultation) involve seances, with whimsical results which are amusing but hardly startling.

Certainly the most delightful of the stories is "El concierto" (The Concert). Narrated in the first person, it relates the experiences of a man whose passion for whistling and development of this talent attract a loyal following among his neighbors, who use their balcony as a "box at the opera." But finally this unusual "artist" is upstaged by a phonograph. The narration is handled with a fine skill for description, not only of the physical surroundings but also of the actual sounds which determine the outcome of this highly original and convincing short story. Another successful tale is "Si yo fuera ladrón" (If I Were a Thief), in which a young man fantasizes about being a robber in what he assumes to be his own apartment, only to discover that he has gotten off the elevator on the wrong floor and entered the rooms of a stranger, leaving his fingerprints behind.

"Aunt Germana" is the most notable achievement in *Unlikely Tales*. It is considerably longer (twenty-eight pages) than any of the preceding stories, and the psychological insights and observations revealed in the development of the eccentricities of the central character are unexpected in the work of so young a writer. The story is narrated in the first person by a nine-year-old boy who describes the growing obsessions and fantasies of his father's widowed and aging aunt. She has come to live in his home, and immediately meddles in the operations of the household. To get attention she complains about her ailments. She collects great quantities of Catholic magazines which she refuses to discard, until one day she inexplicably throws them from her bedroom window. The imaginary ailments increase, and she moves from eccentricity to what appears to be insanity—or at least borderline insanity. She insists that she is being pursued, that attempts are being made on her life, and that the cartoons she sees in the newspapers are thinly disguised attacks on her. Her fantasies are not without humor, for one of her illusions is that the Quintero brothers have been hired to write a play in which she will appear as a character.

The young narrator, who happens to like detective stories, volunteers to aid his great-aunt in seeking out her oppressors. Finally,

Aunt Germana attempts suicide by leaping from an upstairs window, but only succeeds in injuring herself. After a few days, she awakens from a coma, fully convinced that she is dead and that her spirit is in purgatory. She devotes herself to playing the "role" of a ghost at night—or at least her idea of what a ghost should be. In time, the boy's mother finds a solution by recommending that Germana take her "spirit" to a convent where, surrounded by nuns, she would be more likely to get out of purgatory and closer to heaven. The aunt is taken aback by this bit of reasoning but accedes. Her "spirit" finds peace long enough to prepare a will leaving her money to the convent. She refuses to receive visits from her relatives under the pretext that she no longer exists. However, before really dying a few years later, in a moment of "lucidity or confusion," she does set aside a part of her fortune for her long-suffering family and dies without leaving her spirit behind.

"Aunt Germana" is a prose piece of unquestionable literary worth, and it provides evidence of the young author's promise at the earliest stage of his career. The story also clearly anticipates some of the best dramatic works of López Rubio's maturity, in which the role of illusion in human behavior and relationships is a fundamental theme.

II Roque Six

Were it not for Eugenio de Nora's precise and admiring critique of *Roque Six* in his *The Contemporary Spanish Novel*, López Rubio's single novel would be a virtually forgotten book. De Nora calls the work a "small masterpiece of the most unblemished humorism." [2] López Rubio began the novel in 1924, when he was twenty-one, and completed it in 1927. Structurally, it can be identified as a modern variation of the picaresque novel, in which a single antihero (Roque Fernández) moves through a series of five reincarnations very much in the manner in which Lazarillo de Tormes moves from master to master. But whereas Lazarillo's adventures lead to an accommodation with society, Roque's experiences with dying prepare him for a sixth and definitive meeting with death. At the same time, there can be detected in the novel a Pirandellian concern for multiple personality—not only in the various incarnations themselves but also in the fantasy lives invented by Roque during his second life and in his final union with "el otro" (the other).

The novel opens with a description of a sickroom and of the sensations of a man who is dying of pneumonia in Madrid. The death appears real, but the man's consciousness reawakens in another body in Paris (which he recognizes from stereopticon photographs he has seen). His memory begins to sharpen, and in a flashback we learn of Roque Fernández's childhood in Spain with his widowed mother, who was an opera singer by profession. He has attended preparatory school, visited his mother in different hotels, slept in the same bed with her, and has been lavished with affection. In these passages, López Rubio achieves an almost Proustian sense of place in his descriptions of colors, smells, and the feelings of childhood.

As an adult, Roque ends up working in a dull government office. He gets married, has several children, and, with money inherited from his mother, buys himself a motorcycle. One night, after leaving a performance by an amateur theatrical group, he catches pneumonia and experiences his first death. In his second incarnation, he discovers that he speaks French perfectly and that he is Jean Rocherier, employee of the Ministry of Justice, with wife and three small children. López Rubio describes Roque's first nervous night with his new wife with a fine command of humorous suggestion and imagery and a sense of the absurd. But eventually he does adjust quite well to the situation and accepts the "role" of Jean. There are several humorous vignettes which describe Roque-Jean's progress toward his second death. He develops into an habitual liar—or at least an incorrigible inventor of imaginary professions, so that the effect is that of experiencing a series of incarnations-within-an-incarnation. His second death occurs with a touch of absurdity when he chokes to death trying to swallow the ball from a roulette wheel.

In his second reincarnation (and third life), Roque awakens as an English-speaking Protestant minister, the Reverend Farjeón, in the town of Ainsworth, Nebraska. His wife (Edith) is "big, fat, full of compassion and strong as a column." Together they have produced six offspring in nine years. Farjeón is very popular with his flock because he gives good "performances" in the pulpit. Life grows complicated when Roque-Farjeón discovers that the previous inhabitant of Farjeón's body had been having an affair with the cross-eyed Mrs. Fishmonger. He is visited unexpectedly by the mysterious Dimas, who announces that he had been run over by a car the day before in Philadelphia but has been denied entrance into heaven. In this episode, the absurd gives way to the phantasmagorical, and Roque experiences his third death by drowning after being enticed into the water by his reflection. In the previous incarnation he had been revived by artificial respiration after almost drowning, so his predilection for destruction by water had already been established.

The third reincarnation takes Roque to Rumania and plunges him into the political intrigues of eastern Europe. He awakens in a Bucharest jail as Professor Pazandjick, who has been involved in an anarchist plot to assassinate the royal family. Roque protests his innocence, since the crime was committed before he took over the professor's body. There is a detailed escape by Roque-Pazardjick's companions, but he himself remains behind and is executed—crying out and rebelling against his fate at the last moment and turning his back on the firing squad. This is perhaps the most startling episode in the novel. Roque's Kafkaesque predicament and the events of his fourth death are extremely grim, in contrast with the absurdist humor with which death had been treated in the earlier episodes. López Rubio's satirical depiction of a general who comes to power by chance and the underlying contempt for the military mentality would certainly have made *Roque Six* unacceptable for publication had it been written in the years following the Spanish Civil War.

The fourth reincarnation is brief and continues in the grim vein of the preceding episode. Roque is reborn as an almost toothless infant. In the cradle he has his first thoughts of suicide, and he bites his nurse's breast with his single tooth. In anger, the woman grabs the child by the leg and hurls him over the balcony into the street to meet another violent death. Roque's final return is to a strange and unidentifiable land. He is reincarnated with an identical twin—his "other" (otro). They are a kind of Cain and Abel, and the author describes them as "the boy with red boots and the one with black boots." Both love the same girl, and Roque kills his rival and then himself to achieve an end to his reincarnations. He finds a door to enter, and "when he came to die, he had already died a lot before. Half-soul and half-soul were joined together in the air." [3]

In *Roque Six* López Rubio created effective and sometimes memorable descriptions of sensual impressions, and he showed himself capable of dealing with absurdist scenes, mordant satire, and grim reality with equal effectiveness. If the semimystical final episode is somewhat less lucid than the preceding chapters, it cannot be faulted in terms of style. There is, to be sure, a noticeable imbalance in the length and design of the various episodes, but the same relative imbalance can be found in *Lazarillo de Tormes*, which is, to a degree, the prototype for López Rubio's imaginative work.

De Nora correctly describes *Roque Six* as a work of humor, but it must be pointed out that the young author, while influenced by the aesthetics of his Spanish contemporaries, was utilizing a type of dark,

absurdist humor that would be widely cultivated in Western literature some decades after *Roque Six* was written. Given the obvious
merits of this first novel, one may well wonder why López Rubio
never attempted another prose work. But when his other activities
and ambitions of this period are taken into consideration, it is obvious
that the lure of the theater was far too strong for him to combine
indefinitely the dual career of novelist and dramatist. Already he had
made several attempts at collaboration on plays with Jardiel Poncela
and Neville. His and Neville's *Alone at Last* had reached the stage in
1927 as transformed by Honorio Maura into *His Right Hand*. And, in
1928, *Overnight* brought López Rubio (and his collaborator Eduardo
Ugarte) the kind of fame and professional rewards he could never
hope to enjoy as a novelist of avant-garde bent.

III   De la noche a la mañana *(Overnight)*

Of the several attempts López Rubio made at writing plays with
other young dramatists during the late 1920s, only two achieved
productions. Both were the result of a collaboration with Eduardo
Ugarte Pagés, and both were so skillfully crafted that they in no way
betrayed joint authorship. It is entirely possible that their first play,
Overnight, would not have been accepted by a professional management if it had not received the *A B C* award in a contest for new
playwrights in 1928.[4] Theatrical impresarios in Spain have not been
noted for being adventurous in the selection of new works for presentation on their stages, and *Overnight* was an intellectual play of
considerable sophistication, a serious comedy which, for all of its
humor, ended on a somber note. The premiere, on January 17, 1929,
was very successful, and critics were enthusiastic. One observer of
the Madrid theatrical scene wrote: "with rare unanimity the Madrid
theater critics, customarily so antagonistic, have recognized in the
play . . . an essential virtue: novelty of tone, of expression, of
humor with which the authors have approached a dramatic situation. . . ."[5] Within a year the play had been translated into Portu-
guese, Italian, and English; and the appearance of a textbook edition
in the United States in 1934 indicated that this work by two virtually
unknown writers was of sufficient intellectual and literary interest to
justify its publication for academic study.

Considering the play more than two decades after its first performance, Domingo Pérez Minik showed none of the enthusiasm of the
earlier critics. Although he acknowledged the theatrical know-how of

the authors, he found the play structually defective after a good first act, and placed it somewhere between "a false restoration of the *auto sacramental* of Calderón . . . and a belated free interpretation of Pirandello, notably of *Six Characters in Search of an Author*." [6] However, the development of the dramatic action of *Overnight* is far more skillful than Minik maintained; and it seems doubtful that López Rubio and Ugarte were consciously thinking of Calderón when they sat down to write—though evidence of Pirandello's influence can indeed be found in the play.

The action of *Overnight* centers around a crisis in the life of a man (Mateo) who has now reached the *mezzo del cammin* and has become disillusioned about love. In spite of an apparent cynicism, he maintains the illusion that he may still find happiness. His *conciencia* (conscience) exists in the drama as Don Mateo, a man of austere appearance who represents the restraining force on Mateo until being inactivated by the charms of an unusual young woman. The editor of the American edition of the play has pointed out that the Spanish word *conciencia* has a more extensive meaning than the English cognate, and that it includes the power of reasoning as well. She also emphasized that Don Mateo is not simply the symbolic representation of Human Conscience but "as real, as individual as Mateo himself. . . . He is that element in man which sets man apart from the rest of creation, namely his power to reason, to interpret and to judge his own actions." [7] This literary splitting of a personality was not in itself a dramatic innovation. In a discussion of the play after its premiere, Alejandro Miquis noted that a French company had performed, a few months earlier, a work with a similar theatrical device, and that the authors themselves had claimed no originality in their dual representation of the protagonist of *Overnight*. Miquis found the idea attractive, since it had enabled the authors to eliminate all suggestion of soliloquy and to avoid the use of extraneous characters to convey certain information to the audience. [8]

López Rubio and Ugarte set the action of their play in a country house where there is no suggestion of local color or custom that would in any way make the location seem alien to a non-Spanish audience. Certainly the residence of Mateo could just as easily be found outside Paris, or London, or New York. By the same token, the characters reveal no characteristics that would stamp them unmistakably as Spanish. Specific textual directions concerning the stage setting and the appearance of the principals indicate that the playwrights were fully aware of the value of certain exterior aspects of decor and makeup in suggesting the nature of their characters.

When the play begins, Mateo and Don Mateo are on stage together. The opening dialogue is a brief exchange between Mateo and his servant Santiago (who cannot see Don Mateo). The servant has come to inquire if his employer wishes him to close the outside door, for it is after eleven o'clock at night. The playwrights immediately capture the attention and interest of the audience by hinting in the dialogue that Mateo is hoping that someone will arrive, even though it would seem improbable at the late hour with a heavy rain falling. On a different plane of interpretation, the open door and the late hour may be seen to correspond to Mateo's age and lingering hopes. Thus, at an early point in the play, the possibility of two levels of meaning becomes apparent.

After the departure of Santiago from the scene, Mateo and Don Mateo begin a discussion of the former's situation in life. Mateo maintains that he has achieved tranquility and that there is nothing more that he needs. Servants are a buffer between him and the small disturbances of everyday life. Don Mateo replies that there are some things that even a servant who makes an art of his mission cannot supply. For example, there is love (*cariño*, which means deep affection). Mateo then declares that love (*amor*, or passionate love) has only served to embitter his life. There is, of course, an obvious and intended difference in the two Spanish words that is not easy to suggest in English.

Up to this point, Mateo had not been aware that he has been talking with another person, and when he comes to the realization that there is another physical being in the room, he asks his identity. Don Mateo obliges:

DON MATEO. I am your conscience . . . your soul, your reason. Call it what you like. I'm that sounding board that men have for talking with themselves when they're alone. A mirror in which you see yourself. A voice inside you.
MATEO. What? You aren't a man of flesh and blood?
DON MATEO. No. Only a *representation*.[9]

The doorbell rings, and a young woman, drenched with rain, is admitted by Santiago. Her name is Silvia; she is attractive and acts on impulse.[10] It was in this character that Miquis discovered the novelty of *Overnight*. He wrote in his review that she revealed herself as an enemy of logic, or at least she was unconcerned with it: "The new authors have dispensed completely . . . with traditional logic in the theater, which had come to be like a suit of armor, limiting the writer's creative movements enormously. They have not concerned themselves with—perhaps it would be better to say they've fled from—justifying the conduct of the characters in their play." [11]

Silvia's first appearance does have a reasonable explanation. The car in which she had been traveling with her husband, Jacobo, has broken down; however, she is in no hurry to disclose that she has a husband or a vehicle. When the youthful husband arrives looking for her, Silvia hides, and Mateo manages to convince him that she is not in the house without really telling a lie. But Don Mateo is horrified by each new and compromising development. Silvia persuades Mateo to let her stay overnight, and he is surprised to learn that she intends to return to her husband the next day after apparently trying to escape from him:

MATEO. Then you're going to turn back?
SILVIA. Where is back?
MATEO. After you've taken this step! . . . In life one can never turn back.
SILVIA. Why not?
MATEO. Because life moves forward with us.
SILVIA. A streetcar also moves forward, but you can ride backwards in it as well as forward. Because streetcars go and come back.
MATEO. But we can never go back to where we started in life.
SILVIA. Of course you can. Just turn back the clock. . . .[12]

Mateo begins to be fascinated by Silvia's ideas about time and agrees to join her game and pretend that they are once more at the moment of her arrival. She reminds her benefactor that he must also tell Jacobo that she isn't in the house when he appears again. To Mateo's surprise, the bell sounds and Jacobo does reappear. The prospect of spending the night in the automobile has not been too appealing, and he requests lodging from Mateo and is finally permitted to go upstairs to a spare bedroom. Showing no particular concern about his wife's sleeping arrangements, he bids Mateo good night with a significant observation about Silvia's nature:

JACOBO. She lives absurdity with the greatest calm. She makes no distinction between what is logical and what isn't; but she always manages to resolve matters in an unexpected way—unsuspected even to her. . . .

After Silvia has retired to Mateo's bedroom on the first floor, man and his conscience are left alone again. Don Mateo observes that there are *conciencias* that can be bribed; some can even be killed; but in their case it is the *conciencia* that is stronger. It turns out, however, that Don Mateo can be put to sleep, and in a manner that provides an amusing and effective curtain for the first act of the play. Mateo picks up the financial page from a newspaper and begins to read the stock quotations aloud. Don Mateo starts to yawn, and as he falls asleep, Mateo—still reading aloud—makes his way toward the bedroom door.

At the beginning of the second act it is morning, and Mateo and Silvia come onstage from the same bedroom. Don Mateo is distressed, and in order to get Jacobo to the scene as quickly as possible, he writes "Come downstairs" in white chalk on the back of Santiago's jacket. The husband is angry when he discovers his wife in the house, but it is made unmistakably clear to the audience that nothing really happened behind the closed door overnight, probably because outright adultery would have been totally unacceptable on the Spanish stage in 1929, but also, perhaps, because infidelity would have been too logical for Silvia.

Don Mateo accuses Mateo of having an ulterior motive in not sending the young woman off with her spouse, even though she has insisted she doesn't want to leave. Mateo tells his conscience that he, too, would be captivated by this unusual woman if his very nature did not exclude truly passionate involvement. Don Mateo is challenged and reveals that it would be possible for him to become human and undergo a test to discover if he is susceptible to Silvia's peculiar charms. Just as Apuleius recovered his human form by eating a flower, Mateo's conscience can become human by placing a flower in his lapel. When Silvia returns to the scene, she is introduced to a visible Don Mateo who is ready to assume a role in what amounts to a play-within-a-play. Mateo tells her that his friend will take his place as her escort and then excuses himself. Silvia captivates Don Mateo completely. He begins to laugh with her, and his seriousness gives way to utter fancifulness.

Between the second and third acts of *Overnight*, a little more than an hour has elapsed. Silvia returns from a stroll with Don Mateo, who has remained in the garden. Mateo attempts to talk of serious matters, but Silvia refuses to listen and leaves the room. Mateo summons Don Mateo from the garden and, in a climactic scene, they discuss the reaction of the *ex-conciencia* to Silvia's capricious personality. Now Mateo finds himself in a reversed role. He accuses Don Mateo of having taken advantage of Silvia's *inconsciencia* (that is, her incapacity for conscious reasoning) in order to win a kiss. Don Mateo reminds him that he, too, has taken advantage of the same thing, for it was Silvia's *inconsciencia* that made it possible for her to spend the night in a compromising situation. Mateo insists that it was different in his case, that Silvia came because he was waiting for her. The two characters debate their right to possess her. Don Mateo, no longer the stern figure of the first act, tries to bargain with Mateo, who is furious and resorts to the ultimate weapon: removing the flower from his rival's lapel to make him invisible again. This is the moment of greatest intensity in the play, and the authors cleverly interrupt the argument with some typically inconsequential lines spoken offstage by Silvia. And they reveal, with a touch of humor, that Mateo reacts logically at this point whereas Don Mateo's response is illogical:

SILVIA. (*Offstage.*) Mateo, I suppose you'll have strawberries for dessert. . .

MATEO.   Strawberries aren't in season yet. It's February.
SILVIA.   What a shame! I was counting on a dessert to match my dress. . . .
DON MATEO.   Tell her yes! Tell her we'll have strawberries. . . .

Jacobo returns, after having the car repaired, to claim his wife. Mateo is frantic at the idea of losing the woman he considers a part of his destiny. His outburst is so impassioned that Silvia becomes frightened, and his words anticipate his approaching insanity:

MATEO.   I'm not going to be sad anymore! . . . I'm not sad anymore! . . . What do you want me to do? . . . Do you want me to sing? . . . Do you want me to jump up and down on the chairs? . . . Do you want me to paint on a moustache with burnt cork?

Silvia calmly prepares to depart with Jacobo, the person who truly comprehends her nature and knows how to deal with it. As the couple leave, Don Mateo—visible only to Mateo—follows them, shouting that Silvia is his life. Mateo, now almost *inconsciente*, echoes the same line: "You are my life." There is a moment of silence; Santiago appears to inquire how many places he should set for the meal; and Mateo, having lost his power to reason, turns to him with the familiar hand-inside-coat cliché gesture of the insane:

MATEO. . . . A hundred and twenty places, because I'm giving a party in honor of my field marshals . . ., because . . . I am Napoleon!"

Overnight is a remarkable first play, with its well-conceived and theatrically shrewd treatment of the conflict that exists when spontaneity does battle with logic and reason. The dual representation of the protagonist and his *conciencia* is nonrealistic in concept but it is

brought to a level of believable theatrical reality with dialogue of an
exceptionally high quality. Outward action is minimized in the play,
but visual symbols and verbal suggestions are employed to heighten
the meaning of scenes or passages of dialogue, giving the play its
underlying poetic currents. The solution to the overnight encounter
of Mateo–Don Mateo with the supremely illogical and spontaneous
Silvia is neither an acceptable self-realization nor a logical adjust-
ment; rather, it is a definitive turning away from further battle. There
is, to be sure, a quality of deep irony in the transformation of Mateo,
who had arranged his life to avoid the possibilities of disillusionment,
into the mad individual who refuses to accept an existence without a
woman whose only communication with him had been on the level of
the absurd.

IV   La casa de naipes (*The House of Cards*)

In their second play, *The House of Cards*, López Rubio and Ugarte
turned from the highly fanciful to a treatment of realistic characters in
realistic dramatic situations, though not without certain poetic suggestions. The action of the play takes place in a Madrid *pensión*, and
the only nonrealistic element is in the design of the stage setting,
which gives visual meaning to the title of the work. In an *autocrítica*
(the author's own evaluation of a work) which appeared at the time of
the premiere, on May 27, 1930, the playwrights explained the nature
of their drama:

> *The House of Cards* is . . . an ordinary play. Its episodes are intentionally
> commonplace, so that, in contrast with the set, which is the fantastic charac-
> ter, they will have an ironic transcendence, without which we would not have
> wanted to write the play. In *The House of Cards* we sought, seeking
> ourselves, a different direction from *Overnight*. . . . We believe that we have
> created a stronger dramatic work. It remains to be seen if it is a better one.[13]

The stage setting to which the playwrights referred was quite
advanced in design for the Spanish theater of 1930. The properties
and furnishings were totally realistic, but the overall construction was
suggestive rather than literal. A double-level stage (a concept in stage
arrangement that can, of course, be found in various forms throughout theatrical history) permitted the simultaneous presentation of
scenes in two distinct areas of the *pensión* and afforded greater
freedom of movement than the conventional box set. The symbolic
element of the setting could be found in the enormous playing cards

which served as the walls and roof of the house. The critic for *A B C* took note of the authors' attempt to give a visual commentary function to the physical aspects of the production and offered his interpretation of the significance of the cards:

. . . the procedure of reproducing scenically motifs of the card deck as setting and background for the work gives emphasis to and sums up [the play's] idealistic meaning. This symbolic character, which gives a modern aspect to the new production . . . alludes to the hidden magic of the cards. . . . They express hopes, fortune, chance, failed ambitions, beautiful dreams and impossible acts of madness.[14]

In contrast with the illogical or fantastic nature of the characters of *Overnight*, those of *The House of Cards* are recognizable types that, at one time, had counterparts in the *casas de huéspedes* (pensions) of the cities of Spain and other countries. Miquis observed a Galdosian flavor in some of the principals, a quality that is unmistakable in the character of Doña Rita, the owner of the *pensión*.[15] The central theme of the play is illusion and subsequent effect of disillusionment on the lives of the characters. The work clearly anticipates the plays of López Rubio's second career, in which he reveals a continuing concern for the role of illusion in human affairs. In *The House of Cards*, the word *ilusión* recurs frequently, and it is significant that one of the main characters—Alejandro—and his colleagues are circus performers known as *ilusionistas*, or magicians.

The opening act of the play is composed of a series of scenes which serve to introduce all of the characters that figure in the action and to present their interrelationships. Most of these scenes are exchanges of dialogue between two characters, but at the end of the act, all are brought together in an effective dramatic ensemble. Before the action begins, the sound of a piano can be heard, and the practicing continues offstage throughout the first three scenes. The play opens with the arrival of Andrés, a serious student who has come to Madrid to prepare for his university examinations. Doña Rita, a woman of sixty who makes some effort to hide the ravages of time, shows him the facilities of her establishment. Doña Rita displays a dominant behavior characteristic (absent-mindedness) and a dominant obsession (a craving for money), and her absent-mindedness provides an element of humor to the otherwise serious proceedings.

Following a brief scene between Doña Rita and her servant Juana, Don Néstor appears. He is an elderly, impoverished man who rents a room in the boardinghouse and has the obvious function in the play of confidant to several characters, affording them an opportunity to reveal their personalities more fully to the audience. His own particular problem—estrangement from his wife—is introduced briefly in the final act and does not bear directly upon the events of the play. Don Néstor understands Doña Rita's parsimoniousness very well. He knows that she has acquired a new boarder when she gives instructions to the servant to take the bedspread and ashtray from his own room to place in the quarters of the student. He is also aware that she keeps placing advertisements in the newspaper in hope of finding one boarder more.

Doña Rita considers it an indignity to run an establishment for the public and deludes herself with the idea that she will eventually be able to assume a higher position in society. Her daughter, Elena, is being educated as a *señorita*, learning refinements for which she has little talent or interest. Néstor suggests that her time could be spent on more practical learning, but Doña Rita is certain that the girl will marry into a wealthy family. Elena herself is clearly bored with her existence, but she has no dreams of her own to enable her to escape from the artificial life her mother has created for her.

One of the boarders is Alejandro, a thirty-year-old circus performer, who is boastful, talkative, and broad of gesture. He lives for the moment, and Doña Rita finds his extravagant nature appalling. Although seemingly without personal illusions, he is capable of stimulating the illusions of others, and he is keenly aware of the need for fantasy in life. Every action is carried out with a brash confidence that is in striking contrast with the timidity of the student Andrés. The latter lacks any genuine ambition for the law career for which he is studying, and he is taking the exams only because of parental pressure. Both men are attracted to Elena, and a part of her responds to each of them. When Alejandro arrives to celebrate his new contract, Doña Rita's concern for the cost of things prevents her from joining in the festivities and enjoying the champagne the performer has bought. In the presence of all of the boarders, Alejandro breaks an egg into a bowl, pours oil over it, and lights it. Doña Rita fears that he will burn the carpet, but the *ilusionista* is only performing a magical trick. A dove flies out of the bowl, to the delight of all the onlookers except the landlady. Don Néstor, caught up in the excitement, picks up a plate and throws it in the direction of Doña Rita, calling to her to catch it. But she is distracted and lets the plate fall to the floor and shatter.[16] The final line of the scene, spoken by Don Néstor, has not only an immediate meaning but also contains a note of warning and prediction for the future: "You aren't prepared for the unexpected."

At the beginning of the second act of *The House of Cards*, Elena is given a long scene with Andrés, who has fallen in love with her, and a comparable scene with Alejandro, who desires her and wants her to leave with him when he goes to Belgium to fulfill his new contract. In these encounters the two men reveal their natures more fully and the choice that Elena must shortly make is put into relief. Andrés confesses that completing the law examinations is not his greatest ambition, but he does not have the courage to tell Elena that his *ilusión* is to marry her. He expresses only his lack of will and faith in himself:

ANDRÉS. At times there is an instinctive fear of touching happiness with one's hands. . . . The fear of not being able to deal with it, of not deserving it. . . . Also, it's so difficult to make up my mind! To think that I'm gambling everything! . . . And that if I lose, it's final, irremediable. . . . To be always doubting!

Alejandro foresees only a life of dullness and mediocrity for Andrés, a life in which whatever progress he makes will be painfully slow. In his opinion, it would be better to have 5,000 pesetas for one day, to enjoy life deeply, even if it meant having nothing the next day. Being an utterly cynical man without personal illusions, he creates around himself artificial illusions, as false as the sleight of hand that he performs in the circus. He offers Elena an opportunity to escape from the existence that she detests by going away with him but makes no promise of a permanent relationship.

Doña Rita enters in an animated mood. She has lost two of her boarders, but she has devised a new way to deal with her financial woes: she wants Elena to go to work in a glove factory and abandon her studies. The passion for money has dominated Doña Rita to such an extent that she now puts aside her ambition for her daughter to make a socially and financially advantageous marriage. When Elena bursts into tears, her mother cannot understand what has happened until Don Néstor explains to her how she has heedlessly destroyed Elena's illusions. Néstor is aware of the danger and goes to Andrés to urge him to act, to speak to the girl and to give her "a thread of new illusion." Simultaneously, another dialogue takes place on the lower level of the set between Alejandro and Elena. He tells her that he will be waiting in a taxi, and that she must choose either to go with him, resign herself to the life her mother has planned, or accept a conventional life with Andrés. With no support forthcoming from Andrés,

Elena chooses to leave with Alejandro.

The final act of the play was criticized at the time of the premiere because of its repetitiveness, particularly in the scenes in which Doña Rita appears.[17] Shortly after the first performance, certain cuts were made, and in the printed edition of *The House of Cards* the third act is brief and dramatically effective. A month has passed since Elena ran off with the magician, and Andrés has passed his examinations. He has also examined certain papers which Doña Rita thinks will afford her some legal claim to property in Extremadura. They are worthless: another illusion. He then attempts to effect a reconciliation between Don Néstor and his estranged wife, but his efforts result in the destruction of the final illusion that the old man held for escaping loneliness. Alejandro returns in search of Elena, who has left the hotel where they had been living in Barcelona. Doña Rita deplores her daughter's action, for she wants to believe that Alejandro will eventually marry the girl (even though Elena does not love him). The mother shows herself incapable of understanding that Elena has returned to her home with the final illusion that it may still be possible to have Andrés's love. Alejandro convinces her that it is too late, that the memories of the past cannot be expelled. When this dream is destroyed, Elena leaves again with the magician, and the house of cards collapses.

In the published edition of the play there are no stage directions to indicate that the large cards which formed the walls of the setting should fall as a visual symbol of the utter disillusionment that has come to all the principals of the play. But in the original production, the device was employed, and its appropriateness was questioned by Miquis.[18] Certainly the importance of this final visual effect could be debated. *The House of Cards* might be presented in the most conventional stage picture, or with a minimum of stage properties, and still remain a dramatically viable work—in spite of the authors' stated purpose to make the stage setting an integral and ironic element of their drama.

Even though *The House of Cards* deals with more human and realistic characters than those presented by López Rubio and Ugarte in *Overnight*, both plays deal perceptively with illusion and the subsequent effects of disillusionment. In their earlier work, the playwrights elected to reveal the complete change that occurs in the nature of one man during a period of hours; in the second play, the time lapse of a month in each interval between acts permits a more gradual development of complex interrelationships and the presentation of the progressive destruction of Elena's illusions. This concern for the tantalizing effect of the unconventional on people caught in stultifying conventionality links the López Rubio-Ugarte plays to another work of the period that has become a classic of the contemporary Spanish theater: Miguel Mihura's *Three Top Hats*.

By writing a second play of artistic and dramatic worth, with an unfaltering command of theatrical effect, López Rubio and Ugarte had proven that a successful continuation of the collaboration which had produced *Overnight* was possible. But their third play, *Half and Half*, never achieved production, and another proposed collaborative work, *Crac*, was never completed. Both López Rubio and Ugarte accepted contracts to go to the United States to write for the motion pictures, and their further collaboration was limited to a few Spanish adaptations of films for MGM.

CHAPTER 3

The Return to the Theater

I Alberto

THE premiere of *Alberto*, on April 29, 1949, marks the beginning of López Rubio's second career in the theater. The actual writing of the play was done a few years before the dramatist abandoned his cinematic work, during a lull in his activities following the completion of the film *Eugenia de Montijo* in 1944. He had read both *Alberto* and a second play, *Una madeja de lana azul celeste* (A Skein of Sky-Blue Wool) to the director Luis Escobar, who selected the former and more complex work for production in the Teatro María Guerrero. Originally the play had been called *Alfredo*, but before its performance it was rechristened *Alberto*—a name that seems perfectly suited to the imaginary protagonist.

Like *The House of Cards*, *Alberto* is set in a Madrid *pensión*, but the physical characteristics of the establishment show little similiarity to those of the earlier play. Whereas Doña Rita's *casa de huéspedes* was a boardinghouse in the worst sense of the word, this establishment belongs to a higher category and was formerly a private residence of some elegance. In the first act, a crisis has been brought on by the imminent departure of the director of the establishment (Doña Elena) for South America, where she intends to join a man she has loved in her memory for some thirty years. Without her guiding hand, the several individuals who have found in her house an agreeable haven from some of the annoying complexities of modern life will be forced to reestablish themselves and dissolve their present relationships. To avoid the breakup, they decide to invent a fictitious personality to direct their affairs. Each of them will continue to make his financial contribution. The new director is given the name "Alberto," and his creators eagerly set about elaborating on their fantasy.

In writing this play, López Rubio assumed the difficult task of developing credible characterizations for a group of personages who are subscribing to an illusion. In the first act he succeeded marvelously. Structurally, the act is far more complex than any of the scenes which the playwright had attempted in the plays written with Ugarte. In the earlier works, the major part of the dialogue was in the form of confrontations between two characters. These scenes were interrupted or enlarged by the appearance of a third figure, or even a fourth. With the single exception of the final scene of the first act of *The House of Cards*, there was no occasion when a large group of characters had to be manipulated—even in the aforementioned scene, two of the characters were no more than bystanders. In the opening act of *Alberto*, the entire ménage of Doña Elena's *pensión* is presented with consummate skill in a type of dramatic "orchestration" that affords each character his own harmonious expression in the whole. This act, which might well be called the "prologue" of *Alberto*, remains one of López Rubio's prime achievements.

The characters represent several ages and social stations. Doña Elena herself is a middle-aged woman of sentimental nature who harbors the illusion that she may be able to recapture the lost love of her youth. She is, however, the least credible of the play's characters because she is absent in the crucial second act and seems almost an intruder when she reappears in the final act. The first of the boarders introduced is Leticia, a young stenographer with a tendency to speak figuratively and to be carried away by her own sense of the poetical. It is she who actually conceives the plan of inventing Alberto. The antithesis of Leticia is Doña Sofía, an utterly literal-minded woman of sixty-four who is accompanied by her overly sheltered daughter, Elvira. The most forceful of the group is the old Marquesa, who maintains a brow-beaten paid companion, Doña Rosalía. The male contingent is composed of two older men: the loquacious Don José, and Don Pascual, an employee of a government office. Javier, a young dentist who frequents the establishment and is in love with Leticia, completes the group.

These characters are all the more human because of their occasional inconsistencies. Leticia, for all her capacity for illusion, reveals some strikingly realistic insight into the behavior of men and is one of a series of female characters in López Rubio's plays who comment on the egotism and lack of dependability in the opposite sex. Leticia's feeling for the fanciful and imaginative contributes to the air of poetry that the dramatist has given to his play. But always present is the counterbalance of the other guests, who are not without their own weaknesses for illusion even though they prefer to express themselves in a more literal manner. Their reactions to Leticia are a source of humor as well as variety. Javier, who loves the girl, is more understanding of her manner. As he points out, her way of expressing ideas is simply poetry:

JAVIER.   Her way is known as poetry.
THE MARQUESA.   Well, I prefer that people call bread bread and wine wine, even when I don't taste it.
JAVIER.   And poetry is precisely calling bread wine.[1]

The dialogue of the first act is allusive and evocative. Very little of the past lives of the group is revealed through conventional exposition, but a great deal is suggested. For example, a simple line from Doña Sofía is sufficient to indicate something of her relationship with her daughter—that of a possessive mother who has lavished too much affection on a single child and who is determined to keep her a child:

LETICIA.   A little imagination and we are saved . . . A little love, and Alberto is born. . . .
DOÑA SOFÍA.   With love alone?
LETICIA.   We have all been born from love.
DON PASCUAL.   Yes, but in another manner. . . . In reality. . . .
DOÑA SOFÍA.   Don't spell out reality in front of Elvira!

Doña Sofía's words are humorous, of course; but, as is so often the case in the plays of López Rubio, the underlying implications are serious. Later, Elvira's rebellion at accepting Alberto as her imaginary brother who must share the mother's affection gives further suggestion of her abnormal ties to her parent. With a calculated note of irony, the playwright has given the final line of the first act to Doña Sofía, the person who had seemed immune to poetical thought. When Leticia announces that the fully imagined Alberto has just walked out the door, Doña Sofía, after a moment of silence, reveals her complete captivation by the new fantasy: "How extraordinary! And it seems as if he had only arrived. . . ."

After six weeks of life under the "rule" of Alberto, it becomes evident that each of the boarders is attributing his own fancies and the fulfillment of his desires to the mythical landlord. Even the physical aspects of the *pensión* have changed, and some of the furnishings have been replaced by pieces in better taste—Alberto's taste. It is in the liberation of their suppressed ambitions and emotions that the inhabitants of the establishment reveal their inner natures. The character of the Marquesa takes on larger proportions, and along with Don José and Don Pascual she indulges in a lengthy criticism of modern ways. López Rubio has expressed an admiration for the plays of Oscar Wilde, and in the speeches of the Marquesa, in particular, there is a noticeable Wildean flavor. (The affection of Alberto's creators for Bunburying did not go unnoticed at the time of the play's premiere.) The two older men discuss the problems that Spaniards have in governing themselves and present a critical attitude (stronger than one would expect in the regulated theater of 1949) toward certain aspects of their society. To a degree, these and the other characters form a microcosm of Spanish bourgeois society, but this may be a by-product of the playwright's original intent.

For Javier, a disturbing note is Leticia's growing attachment to the nonexistent man who was created by her hyperactive imagination. She has fallen in love with her creation (Pygmalion and Galatea with a reversal of the sexes), and Javier, with a sense of urgency, attempts to explain to her the nature of her involvement and to show her that Alberto, if he really existed, would possess the same weaknesses as other men. At the end of the second act, a new character—called simply "The Other Woman"—arrives in search of Alberto. Since she was not a member of the original "family," the implication is that Alberto had acquired an existence far more real than had been imagined. He has gotten out of hand and has apparently been less than the ideal director that his creators had expected. Two police officers question the Marquesa about Alberto, and the old woman rises to the occasion with comical disdain and delivers a series of pithy observations on law enforcement.

Unexpectedly, Doña Elena returns from America, where she had met with disillusionment (and, by her subjective interpretation, betrayal). She has shown her inability to forgive or to adapt to a situation that does not conform to her illusion. Whatever the need to bring Doña Elena back to the *pensión*, the the attempt of the playwright to reintegrate her into the action of the play is less than satisfactory. The Other Woman calls again, and now she informs Leticia that Alberto has fled and is being sought by the police. Javier pretends to know the woman, but Doña Elena recognizes the deception: she is none other than the young dentist's nurse. Although Javier's "play" had been devised to destroy Leticia's love for Alberto by portraying him as weak and capable of deceit, the cure has had a stunning effect on the girl. *Alberto* ends on Leticia's note of wonderment; she has not truly awakened from her dream.

DOÑA ELENA. That's not the way. Disillusionment doesn't throw a woman into the arms of another man. . . . At times we even develop a liking for disillusionment.
JAVIER. Have I done wrong then?

DOÑA ELENA.   Oh, my boy, don't ask me!
JAVIER.   (*Going to Leticia*) Did I do wrong, Leticia? Did I do wrong to fight
for my own love, a love of flesh and blood . . . a real love? Do you believe I did
wrong?
LETICIA.   I don't know, Javier. . . . I don't know.

The Spanish critic Torrente Ballester maintains that *Alberto* is
plagued by two basic faults.[2] He is of the opinion that the second and
third acts of the play fall short of the efficacy of the first because the
spectator cannot forget that he, too, has been invited to believe in the
existence of a character who is neither seen nor heard and who has
been invented by a group of people for their own convenience.
Torrente's second objection is to the use of a person outside the world
of the *pensión* as a *deus ex machina* to dispose of Alberto when he has
become unmanageable. Perhaps the second objection is reasonable,
but the first seems an overly subjective reaction to López Rubio's
choice of a dramatic situation that requires a special kind of disbelief.
   All of the boarders are, in their individual ways, practioners of the
art of evasion. It is this aspect of their natures that permits essentially
practical-minded people to accept the idea of a nonexistent manager
of their affairs. Don José, as spokesman for the group, states the true
reason for their seeking a retreat in the *pensión* in the first place:

DON JOSÉ.   We are all here because we don't want responsibilities,
because it is easy for us to pay and not think of the cost. . . ."

This work and others in which the flight from reality is a central theme
have been labeled *teatro de evasión* by some critics and have been
dismissed because they appear to avoid major concerns of their time.
But the play between reality and illusion and what might be termed
the re-creation of reality in the theater of José López Rubio cannot be
fully appreciated if they are approached purely in terms of theme and
interpreted solely as products of modern conditions and attitudes. To
appreciate its true essence, this type of theater must be considered in
its rightful relationship to a long literary tradition which can be traced
back three centuries to Cervantes and Calderón, while acknowledg-
ing its obvious debts to Unamuno and Pirandello in the twentieth
century.[3]
   In a study of the nature of theater since Shakespeare, the American
critic Lionel Abel recognized the need for a term to describe a type of
drama that is neither tragedy nor comedy, a type of theater to which
Alberto and several other works of López Rubio belong. He calls it

metatheatre. Abel points out that there is always a fantastic element in the metaplay. "For in this kind of play fantasy is essential, it is what one finds at the heart of reality. In fact, one could say that the metaplay is to ordinary fantasy as tragedy is to melodrama. As in tragedy the misfortunes of the hero must be necessary and accidental, so in the metaplay life *must* be a dream and the *world* must be a stage." [4] The characters of the metaplay are aware of their own theatricality; they participate in plays-within-the play. In Abel's opinion, Calderón's *La vida es sueño* (Life Is a Dream) offers perhaps the most perfect play-within-a-play and is, along with Shakespeare's *The Tempest*, a prime example of metatheatre. Of course, in the modern theater Pirandello's *Six Characters in Search of an Author* is the best-known example of this type of drama, but Abel has convincingly shown that the more recent *The Balcony* of Genet, in which the characters act out roles in a brothel, is essentially in the same long tradition.

Alberto is theater-within-theater, and only in approaching the work as a form of play-within-a-play does a clear understanding of the playwright's purpose become possible. In the first act, the characters—each a "dramatist" in his own right—elect to perform a play in which the protagonist is imaginary. In order to achieve a sense of reality within the fantasy each must contribute to the composition. They are led by Leticia, for she is the dramatist who conceived the play in the first place and suggested its title (*Alberto*). Actually, the first act is a kind of prologue, for the play of *Alberto* cannot begin until the protagonist is invented and has an opportunity to assume a role (albeit unseen) in the second act. Soon each of the boarders is writing his own special play called *Alberto*, but the different plays converge only at certain moments. This accounts for the less unified content of the second act; the characters (the several Albertos) themselves are becoming autonomous.

At the end of Act II, Javier has decided to write a new play called *Alberto* which will be so astounding that it will discredit Leticia's version. Being an outsider, and desperate to undo the situation, his *Alberto* lacks the idealism of the others. At the end of López Rubio's *Alberto*, the plays have been interrupted without having reached a satisfactory conclusion. Doña Elena interrupts Javier's play (a *dea ex machina* like "The Other Woman") and Leticia is half-awakened from her dream-play or love-play of *Alberto*. There is an element of hope in the possibility that Javier and Leticia can find a common vision of reality or, perhaps, a common illusion.

II Celos del aire
(In August We Play the Pyrenees)

Celos del aire (In August We Play the Pyrenees) is the play which
links the second period of López Rubio's dramatic career to his early
period of collaboration with Ugarte. It was the first work that the
playwright undertook independently, and was begun in the United
States in 1935. Sections were added from time to time during the next
few years, and, due to the interest of the actor Guillermo Marín and
the director Cayetano Luca de Tena, the play was finally completed
in 1949. The title of the work was inspired by that of a *comedia
mitológica* by Calderón called *Celos aún del aire matan* (loosely:
Even Imaginary Jealousy Can Kill) and a popular song, "Yo tengo
celos del aire" (I'm Jealous of the Air).[5] As originally conceived, the
plot was somewhat different from its final form. López Rubio's original concept was to have one case of adultery lead to a second case, but
as the writing progressed the idea of the second adultery was put
aside.

The premiere took place on January 25, 1950, in the historic Teatro
Español, some nine months after the opening of *Alberto*. The play
was received with enthusiasm by the public, and its theatrical values,
particularly the sparkling dialogue, elicited warm praise from virtually every critic of the period. Alfredo Marqueríe wrote: "Besides the
impeccable dramatic construction . . . what delights us most about
this work is the high quality and brilliance of its dialogue, a model and
example of how characters on stage can and should talk without losing
fidelity to their respective natures and, at the same time without
falling into trivialities. . . ." [6] Angel Zúñiga, critic for *La Vanguardia*
of Barcelona, made the significant observation that the dialogue did
not possess the naturalness of everyday talk but rather the "naturalness of good theater. . . ." [7] Torrente Ballester, who had been critical of *Alberto*, expressed his admiration for the dramatic skill displ ay-
ed in the contrapuntal design of the work, and his only reservation
concerned the quality of the "jealousy" scene early in the first act.[8]

The setting for the play is a stately country house situated in the
Pyrenees of northern Spain. As in *Overnight*, a feeling of remoteness
is quickly established. Occupying the house are two couples: the
elderly owners (Don Pedro and Doña Aurelia) and a young couple
from Madrid (Bernardo and Cristina) who have rented the estate—or
at least most of it—for the summer. However, there is no direct
communication between the owners and the paying guests, since

they have agreed on a kind of pretense which divides the premises into two worlds and allows the old couple to maintain the illusion of independence. Only in two areas of the house do they actually come into contact, and even there neither couple speaks directly to the other. An old servant named Gervasio recognizes either pair when it is expedient, and serves as an amusing intermediary.

Since the presence of the old people is not immediately explained, their existence might at first seem to be gratuitous. (Theodore Beardsley cites them as examples of illogical characters that can be found in contemporary Spanish drama.) [9] However, the uncertainty about their role is only temporary. Don Pedro and Doña Aurelia do have functions in the play, and in a theatrical sense they are anything but illogical. Not only do they serve as commentators on the action (while pretending to be unseen and unheard) but they also become an actual audience to a dual intrigue that begins when a third couple, Isabel and Enrique, arrive for a visit with Cristina and Bernardo. In the final scene they play an active part in the reconciliation of Cristina and Bernardo without actually abandoning their pretense.

Christina is uncontrollably jealous. Even when she has her husband completely isolated from society she continues to seek grounds for her suspicions. When Enrique, a playwright, arrives with his wife, Isabel, he suggests that Bernado pretend to deceive Cristina with Isabel in order to cure her of her suspicions once and for all. However, it will be unnecessary for Bernardo and Isabel to *pretend*, for in reality they have already been having an affair which Enrique has not suspected. The moment the two are left alone they embrace passionately, providing a surprising and ironical ending for the first act.

The succeeding action takes place the afternoon of the following day. Doña Aurelia and Don Pedro sit in their *butacas* (which in Spanish means both armchairs and theater chairs) at one side as observers, and occasionally they comment on the happenings. Isabel analyzes her husband for Bernardo, explaining his habit of re-creating everything he experiences to suit his own egotistical fancy:

ISABEL. He has too much imagination to notice anything right under his nose. He never reads a book the way other people do. He only looks at the pages and fills in the rest for himself, without bothering about the author's words. When we're talking, he answers questions I haven't asked yet.
BERNARDO. Because he already knows what you're going to say. . . .
ISABEL. Because he prefers to invent what I'm going to say. He never listens to anyone because he's always listening to himself. At concerts he substitutes

the music in his mind for what the musicians are really playing. At the theater
he sees an entirely different play from the one on the stage.
BERNARDO. But he has two eyes. . . .
ISABEL. He always has a mirror in front of his eyes, where he watches
himself . . . day and night.
BERNARDO. And when you make love?
ISABEL. I'm only the reflection of his own passion. When he makes love to
me, he's really making love to himself. . . . [10]

   She explains that as a lover Enrique had played a role that became
boring after their marriage. Until she met Bernardo, Isabel had
resigned herself to the farce, "to take cards in that game that life is for
him. . . ." By using such pointed theatrical references as "farce" and
"game of life," López Rubio is clearly underlining the complete
theatricality of the lives of his characters. Isabel herself is decidely the
most Pirandellian of the group, for she has acquired multiple personalities after her marriage to supply the numerous heroines of her
husband's plays; stage and life for her have become entwined, and
even her *real* infidelity is, ironically, seen as an invention by her
husband and transformed into theater.
   When Enrique has an opportunity to be alone with Cristina, he
succeeds in arousing her suspicions by suggesting that sightseeing is
not the main reason for the walk Isabel and Bernardo have taken
together. But he also begins to have some doubts about the wisdom of
his own plot. Finally, he explains to Cristina that it was only a plan to
make her think she had been deceived, and she, in turn, proposes
that Enrique enact with her the same kind of deception. When
Bernardo's voice is heard from the garden, Cristina moves quickly;
she curls up on the sofa next to Enrique and orders him to talk to her.
When he can think of nothing to say, she tells him to recite the names
of the provinces of Spain in a romantic way. She takes over as
"director", and Bernardo and Isabel enter to witness a scene that is,
to all appearances, considerably more than a friendly conversation.
This final dialogue of the second act of *In August We Play the Pyrenees*
is a delightful combination of nonsense and calculation. Alfredo Marqueríe suggested that López Rubio may have been influenced by a
similar scene in Jardiel Poncela's *Es peligroso asomarse al exterior*
(It's Dangerous to Stick Your Head Out), in which a telephone
directory is read in an amorous fashion. [11] Enrique Vila Selma noted
the similarity to a section of Guareschi's novel *Il marito in collegio*, in
which a character (Camillo) speaks a series of meaningless lines to his
wife's cousin (Robinia) in order to arouse the wife's jealousy. [12] Since

the Jardiel play was performed some years before *Pyrenees*, and the Italian novel first appeared in 1944, the possibility of direct or indirect influence does exist, but this does not in any way detract from the appropriateness of the scene in López Rubio's comedy of pretense nor does it strike a surprising note in a literary world where borrowings as well as coincidences abound on all levels.

At the beginning of the final act, Don Pedro is indisposed and fears that he will miss the developments between the two couples. He sends Gervasio as an emissary to Enrique to request that he bring the "performance" to his bedroom, which "has a balcony door for entrances and exits." Enrique replies that it could be dangerous for the "players" if the old man has some contagious disease. The conversation affords a new opportunity for the insertion of some amusing observations on the theater and its audiences, observations that one critic found extraneous and labeled "useless propaganda." [13] It is, of course, the complaint of a viewer who missed the point, for one of the most obvious attractions of the play is the clever satire of theater and the skillful use of words and phrases which point up the sheer theatricalness of the characters' relationships on almost every level.

Eventually Don Pedro appears to take his customary place with his wife in their *butacas*. Doña Aurelia scolds him for getting out of bed, but the old man replies that he prefers to die in the front row. If there had been some question about the real function of the couple previously, it is now unmistakable that they are the audience for the "plays" that are being enacted by the younger characters. Rather than representing a fantastic or illogical element in the work, they have now become the point of reference for basic reality within the play.

Isabel suspects that the new interest between Cristina and Enrique is only an invented game; she also understands that Bernardo's growing jealousy reveals his real love for his wife and spells the end of her relationship with him. She tells Bernardo that she could be resigned if she lost him to any other woman, but to see him fall in love again with his wife is difficult to accept. She decides that it is time to bow out and urges Enrique to use a customary ruse for cutting short a visit. Before leaving, Isabel presents her ideas on infidelity to Cristina and advises her on the weaknesses of men and the dangers that women must face. Cristina endures her rival's cynicism, for now her doubts have been replaced by unshakable faith in Bernardo. But Isabel has a moment of vengeance before her final exit. Earlier, Cristina had discovered Isabel with Bernardo in the garden engaged in a love scene. She is still not certain whether it was staged for her benefit or played in sincerity; Isabel coldly tells her that it was real.

The final passages of dialogue fall to Don Pedro and Doña Aurelia. They have also faced the problem of deception and doubt, and their devotion has endured. By listening to a retelling of the crisis that had occurred years before in the lives of the old couple, Cristina and Bernardo are able to apply the experience and wisdom of Don Pedro and Doña Aurelia to their own relationship and to realize their essential need for each other. Although the play ends on a cheerful, positive note, there is an underlying seriousness, and even poetry, that lends dignity to the comedy.

The characters in *Pyrenees* are not, of course, fully developed in a psychological sense, but they are masterfully drawn to serve a theatrical purpose. The use of theater to produce theater may call to mind the flamboyantly theatrical intrigues of Molnar's *The Play's the Thing*, but López Rubio has provided recurring moments of genuine human concern that are lacking or glossed over in the Hungarian playwright's Pirandellian exercise in comic intellectual drama. *Pyrenees* established López Rubio's reputation as a leading writer of serious comedy in the postwar Spanish theater and made his name known in parts of Europe and Latin America as well. Even after he had written other works of equal or perhaps superior merit, this play remained a standard for comparison for many Spanish critics and theatergoers.

CHAPTER 4

A Career Develops

I Veinte y cuarenta (*Twenty and Forty*)

L ÓPEZ Rubio's third full-length play of his second career, *Twenty and Forty*, opened on February 8, 1951, at the Teatro Español, with the prominent actor Guillermo Marín in the leading male role. In the customary *autocrítica*, published on the eve of the premiere of a new work, the playwright described *Twenty and Forty* as a simple *comedia*, "whose possible major theme is reduced to the limits of [a writer] who only dares to treat—with extreme care—lesser themes." He added: "The dialogue serves as a conductor of the action, in which I have attempted to capture the air and tone of our time. A simple game [*juego*], played in full view of the audience, without problems and without anguish. . . ." [1] López Rubio frankly admitted that he had avoided probing too deeply into the possible problems arising from a marriage between a worldly man of forty and an intelligent but inexperienced girl of twenty.

The three acts of the play vary in mood, locale, and dramatic effectiveness; but, as critics concurred, the dialogue is unfailingly apt. In a few scenes, it enhances the dramatic situation so effectively that it almost belies the fact that *Twenty and Forty* is one of the playwright's lesser efforts.

The first act is set in the apartment of a prominent motion-picture director (Lorenzo) who is in "the second youth" which begins at forty. As he explains to his friend Julio, "I'm going to live for myself, to lock up my heart and keep it in the library with other classics." [2] It is the evening of the opening of Lorenzo's newest film, and he has decided to end the three-year relationship he has maintained with Berta, an actress. The society which López Rubio presents is that of successful film-makers, with their militant self-interest and continual search for approval. Some pointed observations on the Spanish cinema of the early 1950s occur in the dialogue, and censorship is slyly satirized. Later, a young actress named Suzy (who has some fashionable Amer-

icanisms in her vocabulary) recounts the great success of Lorenzo's
new film, which was "so good that it didn't even seem Spanish."

The loud festivities in Lorenzo's apartment are interrupted by Don
Ernesto, a neighbor, who comes to complain about the noise. When
he recognizes the celebrities in the room, he asks permission to get
autographs for his daughter, Marga, who is a devoted motion-picture
fan. At the very end of the act Marga appears, and Lorenzo is
immediately attracted to her. Aware of the danger, Berta resorts to
the trick, familiar from the movies, of spilling a drink on the dress of
her potential rival. But Marga, for all her youth and innocence, is not
intimidated. She takes the glass from the hand of the actress and
throws the remainder of the drink in her face.

In tempo and mood, the second act is completely different from the
first, where the war of the sexes was being waged and all of the
superficiality of cinematic society was highlighted. The setting is the
apartment of Don Ernesto and his daughter, and the occasion (some
three months after the first meeting of Lorenzo and Marga) is the first
visit of the film director to the home of his future wife. What gives the
situation a particular charm is the introduction of two eccentric and
improbable aunts (Lola and Clotilde), the "widows of Justo Arial."
The old women add a note of whimsical fantasy to a play that had
begun in a completely realistic vein. Anticipating the possibility that
overzealous character actresses might turn the parts into bizarre
caricatures, the playwright specified in the stage directions that they
should not appear ridiculous to the audience. Lola and Clotilde
behave in a manner which John Mason Brown, the late American
drama critic, once described as "daffy sanity." [3] They are well aware
that they appear a little crazy and are quite willing to admit it. In a
long but effective speech, Marga explains to Lorenzo how the title
"widows of Justo Avial" came to be applied to the two women:

MARGA. . . . Justo Avial died forty years ago. . . . He never married
either one of them. He passed them in the street; then he began to linger
outside. Each of them, from her room, would watch him by raising the blind a
little. They both believed the same thing. . . . In reality, he hadn't made up
his mind. And he took his time in making it up. He came to call at my
grandmother's house. Each of them thought that he was interested only in
her. Then he fell ill with pneumonia. They rushed to his bedside . . . he was
unconscious and couldn't make up his mind in "articulo mortis." Suddenly
they felt themselves rivals. . . . And, when he died, they fell into each other's
arms, united in the love of that man. . . . They call them the widows of Justo
Avial. They don't care. Because, in reality, they consider themselves widows

of the man they both loved. . . .
LORENZO. It's a drama. . . .
MARGA. A small drama, that has made them happy. . . .

As Marga has said, the lives of these women are a little play, a re-creation of life according to their own specifications. This theatrical approach to life is further emphasized at the end of the act when Lola places an armchair in an appropriate location, sits down ("as if it were in a theater"), and takes a pair of opera glasses from her purse to watch the love scene between Lorenzo and her niece. These actions, of course, recall the old couple of *In August We Play the Pyrenees* and the play-within-a-play technique favored by López Rubio in the earlier work. Unquestionably, the aunts are remarkable in a theatrical sense, though the appropriateness of their presence in an otherwise more conventionally realistic play could be debated.

Precociously aware of the problems posed by the differences in age and background, Marga contrasts quite eloquently the full life that Lorenzo has led and her own sheltered, uneventful existence. Indeed, Marga appears to be terribly full of wisdom at this point, unlike the starry-eyed autograph hunter who arrived at the end of the first act. Torrente Ballester, in a rather harsh evaluation of *Twenty and Forty*, found this change in Marga, who "for the elegance of her sentences deserves a place in the Royal Spanish Academy," too abrupt and unexplained.[4]

The final act has still another setting: a summer place on the Costa Brava. With Marga's knowledge and acquiescence, Lorenzo continues to maintain his old professional contacts with actresses; however, it is obvious that the young wife is not contented. A jarring event for Marga is the arrival of Don Ernesto to tell her that he has just married his mistress. He speaks soberly about his dissatisfaction with contemporary society and its moral attitudes.

DON ERNESTO. Today everything is treated as a game. Passion has been eliminated. The heart counts for nothing. And easy infidelity, neither as joke or for real, is considered the logical consequence of love. . . . Believe me, my child. . . . Halfway is no good. Even sinning should be done with conviction. . . .

Lola and Clotilde appear—now driving their own car—to play a role in curing their niece's marital malaise. With some intrigue, the husband of forty and the wife of twenty are brought closer together in mutual understanding, in an ending which might be called "optimistic" rather than "happy." The final act of the play lacks cohesiveness, and although the ending itself is completely plausible, it is impossible to avoid the impression that the events leading to it are overly contrived. When compared with the two plays by López Rubio that immediately preceded it, or with the important serious comedies that were produced a few years later, *Twenty and Forty* seems a decidedly minor work. Ultimately, the dramatic effectiveness of a number of individual scenes cannot completely disguise the unevenness of the play, with its abrupt shift of mood and less than compelling resolution.

II   Cena de Navidad *(Christmas Dinner)*

Cena de Navidad (Christmas Dinner), first performed on November 14, 1951, is another play which fell short of its dramatic possibilities and which did not enjoy a notable success. However, Sainz de Robles, in his annual survey of the theatrical season, praised the first act as example of López Rubio's best dramatic writing,[5] and the playwright himself has expressed his personal satisfaction with the second act.[6] Not unexpectedly, the dialogue of the play received its share of praise. But following the performance of *Christmas Dinner* in Barcelona, a few months after the Madrid premiere, Julio Coll delivered a completely negative opinion—not only of the play in question (which he never got around to analyzing) but of all of López Rubio's theater as well. His harsh attack illustrates the degree of polarization of Spanish critical opinion that was taking place in the post–Civil War period.

What is bad about his theater is that his characters hate exaltation, material misery bothers them, they repudiate the outcry and, all of them . . . practice the difficult art of being inconveniently elegant. I believe that at heart all his characters have in them a bit of "snob." His theater, by dint of being elegant, refined and distinguished, ends up in pure asepsis. . . .[7]

Coll's criticism was obviously opinionated and made no distinctions between the sophisticated or poetic moods of *Celos del aire*, or *Twenty and Forty*, and the very different atmosphere of the play he was supposedly criticizing. Actually, in writing *Christmas Dinner*, López Rubio was creating a less intellectualized type of play, in which the development of suspense and emotional tension are more clearly a part of his dramatic purpose than in his earlier dramas. Also, the dialogue is decidedly less epigrammatic and satirical, though still touched with irony. The playwright had treated the theme of marital infidelity before, and the two principal figures in the marital crisis of *Christmas Dinner* are not unlike those in *Celos del aire* in terms of social station and background; however, the similarities end there.

The Christmas dinner, which gives the work its title, has been announced in a newspaper advertisement which extends an invitation to any person happening to be alone on Christmas Eve without friends or family. The use of some type of public accommodation—a restaurant, a bar, an ocean liner, or even a stagecoach—for justifying the presence of a group of diverse characters for dramatic or novelistic purposes is commonplace. In the modern theater, playwrights of every bent have utilized the device.[8] López Rubio elected to work with a more limited group than the particular situation would seem to suggest. Undoubtedly, the first act—and perhaps the entire play—is weakened because two of the characters (called "The Good Woman" and "The Gentleman") who appear as a result of the advertisement are seen only briefly and do not play significant roles in the drama. Only three persons actually share the dinner: Gabriel (who placed the newspaper notice), Laura (a young woman who turns out to be Gabriel's wife), and Don Juan (an aging cynic who wanted to escape from the usual family rituals). At the beginning of the second act, a fourth figure joins the group: a prostitute referred to as "La mala mujer" (The Bad Woman).

Some parallels can be seen between the plight of the "Good Woman" of the first act and the biblical story of Mary and Joseph in Bethlehem. She and her husband have been unable to find lodgings for themselves and their child and are in financial straits. The fact that Don Juan is the person whom the husband of the Good Woman hopes to contact for a job is an improbable coincidence. Although their small drama is no more than a sentimental interlude which contributes nothing really substantial to the dramatic action of the play, it does serve to reveal something significant about Gabriel. The rejection of the woman is, in a sense, the rejection of humanity (and, consequently, a kind of *evasión*). Gabriel tells Don Juan: "We have come together to cure ourselves with the sorrow of others." [9] Ironically, he is insensitive to the real meaning behind the traditional *cena de Navidad*.

The outspoken Don Juan, who declares that he has neither illusions or disillusionment in his life, is a well-drawn character, and at the end of the second act he resembles a tempting demon, giving cynical advice to Laura:

DON JUAN.   . . . Seek happiness, or whatever resembles it. Live your life. . . . The love of an hour, if you fill up the sixty minutes, is worth more than eternal love without guarantees. Take advantage of the freedom you have in your hands. Who wouldn't change places with you! Don't be like those people who are unprepared when freedom comes unannounced and don't know what to do with it. I have dreamed of it so much that I even have schedules of all the trains noted down, the names of hotels . . . the names of wines. And the phrases of love, well rehearsed, so that they won't fail me when I need them. Enjoy it all, quickly, without waiting for your change. Keeping your heart—which is what kills—as intact as possible, even though to keep it strong you may have to nourish it on the hearts of others. . . .

Then the Bad Woman is given her moment of theatrical grandeur when she cautions Laura against Don Juan's philosophy and relates her own bitter experience with men; noting that "an open door may not be freedom at all—just the entrance to a bigger jail."

In order to present the story of Laura's discovery of her husband's infidelity and separation from him, López Rubio utilizes a clever play-within-a-play in which Laura reenacts the events, with the prostitute performing the role of Julia, Laura's friend. Later, in a theatrically effective reversal of roles, Laura becomes Julia and the Bad Woman assumes the part of Laura. Don Juan takes on the function of director, and finally, Laura returns to the original role of herself.

In the last act, Laura's cousin (Gustavo) appears in an inebriated condition. Don Juan and the Bad Woman believe that he is the wayward husband, but it soon becomes evident that Gabriel is the real spouse. It is probable that many viewers of *Christmas Dinner* suspected the true relationship between Gabriel and Laura before it was actually disclosed. Torrente Ballester, in his critique of the play, remarked on the unnecessary introduction of a new character in the third act and suggested that perhaps the entire final act was superfluous.[10] Without question the second act of *Christmas Dinner* contains the most effective writing to be found in this play, for here López Rubio has an opportunity to present life theatricalized and reality colored by illusion, in the play-within-a-play formula which he handles so skillfully. It is inevitable that Laura's artificial but theatrically purposeful recreation of her past proves more interesting and credible than the final revelation that Gabriel is her husband.

III   Una madeja de lana azul celeste
(*A Skein of Sky-Blue Wool*)

A Skein of Sky-Blue Wool, written in 1947 and first performed in Valencia on October 17, 1951, had its Madrid premiere on December 7, 1951, less than a month after the opening of *Christmas Dinner*. López Rubio himself succinctly described the play: "Four short acts, seven characters and a single, light dramatic situation. . . . This comedy does not aspire to any objective other than an easy one, nor does it expect from the audience anything more or less than the collaboration of an intelligent smile." [11] It served as a starring vehicle for Tina Gascó who, according to the author, lent "the best of her magnificent art to the most difficult and complex character [Lucrecia]." [12] Sergio Nerva wrote that her performance was "one more triumph as a woman and as an actress in these decisive theatrical times in which there are . . . many women and few, very few actresses." [13] Along with *Twenty and Forty* and *Christmas Dinner*, the play was written off as a negligible work by Victor Pradera,[14] but Marqueríe, in a somewhat more considered review, found evidence of the author's skills in the dialogue as well as in the overall mood of the play.[15]

The action of *A Skein of Sky-Blue Wool* is simple and direct. Only in the rather complex character of "the other woman" (Lucrecia) does the work provide a degree of psychological development. In the brief opening act, the wedded bliss of Clara and Daniel, who are still living a prolonged honeymoon after many months of marriage, is threatened by the arrival of Lucrecia, a sophisticated and relentless friend of Clara's who is curious to find out if Daniel is still happy. Lucrecia is "a woman who seems to have fulfilled none of her illusions, for which reason she cultivates a studied audacity and impertinence." [16] There is no doubt that she is looking for some justification for taking Daniel away from his wife. In a scene in which she recalls how she and Clara had met Daniel in Switzerland, Lucrecia reveals elements of her background which help to make her personality and behavior credible and suggest an underlying neurosis.

Clara senses the danger immediately and turns to her sympathetic father-in-law (Marcelo) for moral support and advice. A worldly widower, he has some understanding of the tactics of women like Lucrecia who are driven by their own emotional failures to seek the protection of "philanthropic societies, dogs, musical circles, or, simply, of men." And he observes: "No man can resist them . . . no man can resist the agreeable idea of not being understood and, consequently of being a genius and a child at the same time. No one, not even God, can refuse to let himself be adored."

In the second act, Clara and Lucrecia discuss in more detail their relationship in Switzerland, and it is explained how Clara and Daniel met and fell in love, and how Lucrecia (from her point of view) lost a potential husband to Clara. Actually, what Lucrecia had taken for fascination on Daniel's part had been his way of showing (or trying not to show) his boredom with her. After a week, Lucrecia has taken over many of the duties of a wife and more than a few of a mother. She pampers Daniel excessively and succeeds in annoying Clara.

A new threat appears in the person of Diana, a neighbor who has an older husband and who has shown interest in Daniel. Finally, Clara decides to enter into combat against her enemies with a new weapon. She asks Marcelo to bring her a skein of sky-blue wool. When Daniel discovers a blue bootee which Clara has been knitting, he assumes that his wife is pregnant. The sight of the bootee also has its effect on Lucrecia. After enlightening Diana and sending her home, Lucrecia transfers her romantic interest to Daniel's father, who knows exactly how to deal with her. Clara is not actually pregnant; she has created an illusion through suggestion, but she hopes to make the illusion a reality as quickly as possible. Marcelo leaves his son and daughter-in-law to follow Lucrecia to Naples, and the play ends happily.

With *A Skein of Sky-Blue Wool*, López Rubio attempted to create nothing more than an entertaining romantic comedy suitable for an attentive but undemanding audience. He did not depart in the slightest from the aim stated in his *autocrítica*, and the play provides none of the unleashed fantasy, the theatricalization of life, or the poetic reality that are basic to the finer serious comedies that were completed after this minor work.

IV   El remedio en la memoria *(Remedy in Memory)*

Although there were differences of opinion about the dramatic and literary values of *Remedy in Memory* after its opening in November 1952, it was unquestionably López Rubio's most important work since *Celos del aire*. Torrente Ballester praised the construction of the play as well as its dialogue:

Pepe López Rubio has achieved a hit. And one asks himself why the [success] of the other earlier plays has not been so rotund. Certainly, a total answer would be impossible, for if it could be provided, there would be no failures in the theater. But, in certain relative terms, something can be said. López Rubio possesses excellent qualities as a man of the theater. Some of them he uses on every occasion, such as his gift for dialogue; others, such as his skill for construction, not always. To say that the dialogue of *Remedy in Memory* is perfection is only recognizing something that was expected. . . . But it is also appropriate to insist on the literary quality of this play.[17]

Alfredo Marquerie later wrote: "The psychological study of all that the protagonist thinks, does, says, and feels belongs to the most perfect and finished work of this playwright."[18] Rafael Vázquez Zamora, in a personal interview with López Rubio in the spring of 1953, declared that in his opinion the work was the best play the dramatist had produced at that time.[19]

In spite of such general praise, *Remedy in Memory* has been, perhaps, the least-appreciated of López Rubio's more important plays. The author expressed some pique at the lack of critical perception with which the work was received: "It seemed too subtle and complicated. Scarcely any critic was able to see the double play of fiction and reality, of theater within theater. . . . It's curious; they ask you not to be superficial and, when you stop being, they throw it up to you."[20] The accomplished actress Tina Gascó, for whom *Remedy in Memory* was conceived and written, essayed the exacting leading role, and in the opinion of one critic was unable to sustain adequately the intricate play between reality and illusion which the part presents.[21] Certainly the role is an extraordinarily complex one, and if the leading performer did not successfully convey the sometimes subtle shifts from one level of reality to a "theatrical reality," then it should not be surprising that critics failed to see all the merits of this play.

The theme of *Remedy in Memory* is the substitution of illusion for reality or, as Valbuena Prat expressed it, the "falsification of true reality by an actress, a woman in love, and a mother, by living too deeply the . . . dialogued life of the theater."[22] The protagonist of the play, Gloria Velarde, is a famous actress whose private life is colored by the artificiality and illusion of her professional work. In her moment of personal crisis she must resort to the familiar devices and lines of the theater to deal with her problems. Pirandello had explored the effects of a theatrical career on the private life of an actress in *Trovarsi* (1932), and the mingling of life and theater in drama can be traced far back into theatrical history. However, López Rubio remarked at the time of the premiere that though the theme of his play was hardly new, his approach to the theme was original.[23]

Since the dramatist had already revealed a special concern for the role of consciously or unconsciously created illusion in human affairs and had also spent many years in contact with professional people of the stage and film (where illusion is a daily occupation), it is not surprising that he achieved one of his most complete characterizations in the figure of Gloria Velarde. In all probability Gloria is a composite of many actresses the playwright had known. The comments that López Rubio made on the genesis of his characters in an article in the theater review *Teatro* in 1953 are worthy of consideration, for they provide insight into one aspect of his creative art:

If one is sincere—and he'd probably be a bad writer if he weren't faithful, always, to himself in the length and breadth of his career—he will confess that rarely does a character emerge, whole and true, from reality; that almost never is a character an individual reproduced with complete exactitude.

A character, when he is born and outlined, with a precision that surprises his very creator, is made of many living beings, of many gestures. He may be a synthesis, a distillation, the essence of all that has happened to the author across the years, at different times and places, distant from one another, joined with what he puts of himself, when he creates them, interpreter of what . . . memory or impression has left in him and which may sleep, incomplete, almost unnoticed. . . .

Every human entity leaves something of itself in the soul of a writer, often without his noticing it or seeking it out. . . . For the creator of spectacles, the world is the most complete, varied, and constant of all spectacles. The reality that surrounds him is his own private theater, and his prime activity, as was the case with Mr. Pickwick, is the observation of human nature. . . .[24]

From the opening scene of *Remedy in Memory*, the person of Gloria Velarde dominates the action of the play, even though she does not immediately appear. López Rubio first suggests to the audience something of the vanity of his protagonist and her relationship with her daughter (Luz María) through a purely visual device. Virginia, a retired actress who has become a kind of guardian for the daughter, is placing photographs of Gloria in conspicious locations around the living room of a country house. Luz María enters, and, seeing the pictures of her mother in various theatrical poses, proceeds to remove them. They are for her a symbol of the career which has deprived her of genuine parental love. To Gloria, however, they are symbols of success and of the admiration she has enjoyed. In a few moments, Gerardo, a middle-aged man who is, significantly, a playwright, arrives at the house. He is drawn very much in the image of López Rubio himself,[25] and functions as a confidant for both Gloria and Luz María. Torrente Ballester describes Gerardo as "a bit of the voice of conscience, a type of 'Pepito Grillo' for the central character who enables her to understand herself, the other characters and the audience to understand her." [26]

Before Gloria's actual appearance, she is described by the two people (Virginia and Gerardo) who know her best. From her own personal experience, Virginia knows the falseness of theatrical glamour and speaks to Luz María of her mother's "image" with some cynicism. She suggests that she is eternally playing the "role" of Gloria Velarde because it has become easier than maintaining a double identity. Throughout the three acts of the play, Virginia's candid remarks supply an element of comic relief, although underlying her comments can be detected a note of seriousness. Gerardo shows a more penetrating and objective view of Gloria's relationship to the art of performance, and he provides a key to the understanding of the actress's subsequent behavior:

GERARDO. There are two ways of being sincere—saying what is felt or feeling what is said, putting into it such passion . . . such sudden conviction, that for a moment it becomes true. . . . Theater is pretending, knowing that one is pretending, with intonation correct and posture calculated. The marvel of Gloria Velarde is that she has never gone on stage to act but to live other lives, to believe totally what she is saying, as if possessed. It may be that she lacks the talent to create for herself a character beforehand, that she is incapable of study and reflection. But put her into the situation, supply the words for her, and the creative process begins . . . laughter is born in her or tears burst forth, because what is happening onstage is really happening to her. . . .
LUZ MARÍA. That's all fine for the theater, but life's something else.
GERARDO. Who can pinpoint in an actor where theater ends and life begins? [27]

Gloria shows an extraordinary capacity for making illusion seem reality, but the reality of her own existence is replaced by illusion. For her first entrance, López Rubio employs a favorite device of the theater for introducing the leading actress: having her appear on a stairway (and automatically upstaging whoever else is on the stage at the moment). This theatrical cliché has not been used carelessly in *Remedy in Memory*, for it is completely in keeping with Gloria's character and subsequent actions to enter *reality* in exactly the same manner that she has appeared so often in the theater. The utter theatricality of the actress's nature, which has already been pointed out in the dialogue in which she has been discussed, is now conveyed in visual action.

During Luz María's childhood and adolescence, there had been no genuine communication between mother and daughter, and the girl developed along intellectual paths which separate her even more from Gloria. Although she is a brilliant actress, the mother has little understanding of other forms of creativity, and the books which Luz María reads and the serious music she listens to hold no interest for Gloria. At the end of the first act, Gloria is faced with the startling revelation that her daughter is in love with Antonio, a man who is twice her age and who had actually been the actress's lover many years before. She refuses to accept the reality of the situation and takes a bottle of sleeping pills (which prove to be only aspirin, substituted by the watchful Virginia).

Luz María returns with Antonio, still unaware of the reason for her mother's attempted suicide. She leaves Antonio alone, and Gloria makes a calculated and theatrical attempt to exert her own charms. Antonio explains to her why it was and continues to be impossible for them to have a relationship: "What couldn't be then is even less possible now. Your double life made me run away from you. I saw that you never would be completely mine, because you belonged to the theater. . . ." Then Gloria attempts to convince Antonio that he is too old for Luz María, but he is not shaken in his belief in the love he has been offered. The actress begins to cry and delivers a melodramatic speech based on a role she has played. She is left perplexed when Antonio (her audience), aware of the source of her words, walks away quite calmly. Almost immediately, she is forced to resume the role of "Gloria Velarde" by the entrance of Margarita, an aspiring young actress who has been seeking an interview. Gloria pretends to be interested and asks the girl to learn a particular scene for an audition the following day. Then she delivers a speech on the "religion" of the theater—which she considers an appropriate response for a great lady of the stage. Virginia discovers Gloria still caught up in the illusion of her "scene" with Margarita. She suggests that the actress go to bed, but before being brought back to reality, Gloria answers her as if in a dream:

GLORIA.   Wait. The act isn't over. . . . we still haven't done the scene with the daughter. . . .
VIRGINIA.   (*Surprised*) What daughter?
GLORIA.   (*As if waking up, with effort.*) What did you say?

When Luz María reappears and informs her mother that Antonio has told her all the facts of his past, and that nothing can shake her love for him, Gloria turns without hesitation to the theater for another card to play. She hints dramatically that Antonio is really the girl's father. Horrified by her mother's words, Luz María leaves the room, and Virginia reproachfully demands that Gloria explain what she has done. Again the actress seems to be awakening from a kind of trance. She has just performed the first of her "lies"; however, in her dehumanized state, it ceases to be a question of truth or untruth. As Fernández Cuenca noted,[28] at this point Gloria can no longer distinguish between life and theater.

Margarita returns the following day to perform the scene she has memorized. Gloria instructs her to substitute "Antonio" for the original name "Luis" in the monologue. She is plotting to stage her second "lie" but with no more sense of wrong than that of a director who is manipulating his actors. Luz María has spent the night away from home, but Gerardo brings her back and explains that her mother lied about Antonio. Gloria summons Margarita to perform her audition monologue; however, the girl shows little talent for making bad, outmoded theater believable. She falters and forgets to make the substitution of names. Luz María is appalled that her mother would try to convince her that Antonio had fathered an illegitimate child, but Gloria attempts to sway her with a sentimental speech. When this fails too, she makes a final effort to regain Antonio before Gerardo intercedes. He undertakes to explain to Gloria the meaning of what she has done, of how she has sought "remedy in memory" and has turned to the theater (and not very good theater at that) to avoid "reality."

The play ends with Gerardo expressing a note of hope for Gloria, and the consolation that he, himself, has long loved her—though not so blindly as to risk marriage. Sensing the best way to convince her of the impracticability of their union, he adds: "Furthermore, it would be a bad ending for a play." Although this final scene of *Remedy in Memory* would no doubt cause audiences to react with smiles, it is not a "happy" ending. The light touch of humor is achieved through irony, and the scene also inspires what Abel has called "speculative sadness" in his discussion of the metaplay.[29] The ending may seem to be a backing away from the possible implications of the theme, but it is both logical and dramatically purposeful within the limits the playwright has set. Indeed, a more impassioned or darker outcome would have deprived the drama of the effective contrast with the theatrical frenzy exhibited by Gloria in her attempts to prevent her daughter's marriage. The actress is not destroyed by her incapacity for facing life except in terms of a theatrical re-creation; rather her re-creation offstage fails, and she is ready to return to the real theater, which can also be her salvation.

Remedy in Memory is one of López Rubio's most ambitious works and one that is extremely difficult to perform successfully, since Gloria Velarde's melodramatic excesses are reflections or distortions of roles she has played and are drawn in desperation out of their original context, standing in marked contrast to the measured and intelligent responses of the characters who are not participating in her plays-within-a-play. The playwright obviously did not intend to make the actress a deeply tragic figure, but she is one of his most skillfully developed and complex characters—and probably the first in his plays who is more interesting than the lines she speaks and who acquires an existence that begins before her physical appearance and projects beyond the final curtain.

CHAPTER 5

Two Distinctive Serious Comedies

I   La venda en los ojos *(The Blindfold)*

BETWEEN November 1952 (the time of the production of *Remedy in Memory*), and November 1954 (the opening of *The Other Shore*), López Rubio's career enjoyed a period of artistic ascendency. Discounting the unevenly written and poorly received *Cuenta nueva* (A New Account), the serious comedies produced during the two-year period rank among his best works. Both *The Blindfold*, first performed on March 3, 1954, and *The Other Shore* elicited the warmest critical praise. After the premiere of the former, the reviewer for *El Alcázar* wrote:

José López Rubio has written a most beautiful play. From the first scene to the last there is nothing . . . that is in excess or that is missing. The first two acts are a model of humoristic theater which, approaching farce and even a comic game, carry the spectator to the final stage of the third act with its dramatic, profound and moving turn. . . . The applause and the laughter of the audience were constant throughout the performance, and at the end the curtain rose innumerable times in honor of López Rubio and the cast of the play.[1]

In the opinion of Carlos Fernández Cuenca, *The Blindfold* was one of the best of contemporary plays,[2] and Torrente Ballester stated that in his judgment it was López Rubio's best work.[3] When the comedy was performed in Barcelona in 1956, Enrique Sordo gave it an equally enthusiastic appraisal.[4] Even more recent critiques by observers less sympathetic to López Rubio's theater as a whole have acknowledged the merits of this fine serious comedy. Ruiz Ramón considers it the playwright's best effort and "an excellent piece . . . in the best tradition of the humoristic theater of Jardiel Poncela and the early Mihura."[5] And William Giuliano calls the play "a first-class work."[6] *The Blindfold* has also shown a healthy durability. It was revived in

1963 and published in a college text edition in 1966. In 1973 it was successfully adapted for Spanish television; and, in August 1977, it became the first play by López Rubio to be given a professional production in the United States.[7]

In writing *The Blindfold*, López Rubio allowed his imagination full play and created what is probably his most affecting play as well as an outstanding example of comic-serious theater. Again he chose to deal with the abandonment of reality for illusion, but in a highly original and complex manner. In *Remedy in Memory*, he had treated the case of a woman who was unable to distinguish between reality and illusion—or, more specifically, between reality and theater. In *The Blindfold*, the playwright went further and presented a protagonist (Beatriz) who, abetted by her aunt and uncle, consciously and deliberately denies the existence of chronological time and creates a very special world of illusion. But whereas illusion failed for Gloria Velarde in the earlier play, for Beatriz it provides an acceptable substitute for a reality that she finds inadmissible; and, ultimately, it provides an escape toward a more authentic existence.

The Blindfold begins with a highly imaginative comic twist. The opening scene, in which a female servant (Emilia) relates to a younger girl (Carmen) newly arrived from the provinces the scandalous things she has observed, appears at first to have been devised for exposition of the most conventional kind. However, Emilia later discloses that she has been talking about her *former* employers, and the audience realizes that nothing that has been said in the first five minutes of the play has the slightest thing to do with what is to follow. As Fernández Cuenca has pointed out, López Rubio is satirizing a theatrical cliché as well as abandoning conventional theatrical logic.[8] It is an inspired introduction to a play in which the unexpected is the norm.

Before the conversation between the two servants can move into the affairs of the present situation, Carolina, the elderly aunt of the protagonist, appears and casually asks Emilia if she has told the new girl that everyone in the house is utterly mad.[9] Emilia calmly replies that she'd been about to supply that information when her mistress entered. Carolina then directs Carmen to prepare the bedroom for Master Eugene, because her niece has gone to the airport at Barajas to meet him. From Emilia's gestures to Carmen indicating that she should ignore the instructions, the audience can deduce that Eugene will not actually be arriving.

Ten years earlier, he had failed to return to Beatriz, but she has continued to meet the plane each morning as if no time had elapsed. The aunt and uncle (Gerard) are collaborators, and have invented a world of imagination and fantasy in their comfortable apartment. Carolina dresses up and performs "roles" that she has drawn from novels or her imagination—some days she is Lady Agatha Bresford, and other times she is an international spy or an opera contralto. Gerard's favorite project is placing advertisements in the newspapers to attract people to the apartment—not to sell them anything, but to provide company for the day or an audience for their "performances." His latest notice offered for sale an original Ming vase (which, as he well knows, is a cheap and vulgar imitation). The desired result is achieved when the man referred to as "The Buyer" (*El Comprador*) arrives and remains as a fascinated observer of the events of most of the play. Uncle Gerard also collects autographs, but not of famous people. Rather he prefers the signatures of "unknowns," such as the one he displays of a certain José López. When Carolina appears in the role of Lady Agatha, The Buyer addresses her in English; and, of course, she doesn't understand a word.[10] The whimsical scene is interrupted by the arrival of Beatriz, who engages in a long telephone monologue with her supposedly imaginary friend Julia. (It is in *The Blindfold* that López Rubio first employs the telephone for more than a routine dramatic purpose; in subsequent plays the instrument is used in varied and imaginative ways, so that it could almost be considered a trademark of much of his theater.)

The aunt and uncle assume that "Julia" is only a creation of their niece's fantasy, but later she proves to be a real, though silent, collaborator. When the long monologue ends and Beatriz exits, Gerard and Carolina begin a joint narration of the "drama" of Beatriz and explain how they themselves became a part of the illusion to protect her. Somewhat carried away by the theatrical possibilities of the story, the aunt adds some sentimental touches which her husband reminds her are in poor taste (*cursi*) and out of fashion. Repeatedly the references to theater or roles in the dialogue reveal that both characters are keenly aware of their own theatricality and of the effect of theater on life. Of course, Carolina's multiple personalities are only one indication of the Pirandellian concepts that are fundamental to the play.

Beatriz returns shortly with a new Eugene, whom she has met in the street. This is a turn of events for which the old people are unprepared. Up to this point, the game had followed certain rules and had remained harmless (if bizarre); now Beatriz has invited a complete stranger into the house and appears ready to accept him as her husband. In the second act, Beatriz makes another call to "Julia" to tell her of "Eugene's" arrival. She denies the story she had related the previous day, creating a new version of her "reality." But underneath the stream of feminine chatter can be detected something of the longing and desperation which Beatriz has been hiding for ten years; and she hints to the audience that she is not actually out of her mind. Many of her words contain an unmistakable irony, as, for example, the statement that she loves Eugene "madly" (*con locura*), and the comment that the eight days he has been in Barcelona (according to her new version of events) have seemed like ten years.

Carolina's chief concern has now become the protection of Beatriz from the substitute "Eugene" (Villalba). Although her role of the day is that of international spy, she maintains close contact with reality when she is speaking to Villalba, and she assures him that she is not insane: "It's the effect of the role I'm playing . . . dressed up like a grotesque thing." She is determined that the new Eugene will not take advantage of the role he has assumed in her niece's imagination:

AUNT CAROLINA.   One day she's going to realize that you aren't Eugene.
VILLALBA.   That day I'll stop being Eugene automatically. . . . I'll say that I got off at the wrong floor.
AUNT CAROLINA.   Beatriz has a blindfold over her eyes. It keeps her from seeing clearly.
VILLALBA.   That blindfold can also be love. . . .

Villalba refuses to destroy Beatriz's new happiness by declaring that he is not Eugene. Beatriz interrupts the conversation and insists that her aunt do her spying in another part of the house. When they are alone, she tells Villalba how she has continually renewed her love and how she desires to relive the happiness of her honeymoon. He tenderly joins her in her reinterpretation of the past:

BEATRIZ.   You don't remember anything.
VILLALBA.   But I do, dear. It's just that. . . .
BEATRIZ.   It doesn't matter. People live on memories when they're not really living at all. Now everything is going to be new. As if we'd only just met each other yesterday. What matters is that each new hour begins and we have life before us. I'll bet you haven't even thought of me the last few days.
VILLALBA.   Rather than thinking of you, I was dreaming of you.
BEATRIZ.   That's even better. I also dreamed of you in order not to stop loving you. So that while still being the same man you would seem like another to me. . . .

Beatriz describes her honeymoon as if she were reliving it, and the stage directions indicate that she should go beyond mere narration and *act* the events she is remembering. López Rubio does not permit the love scene to lapse into sentimental excesses, and at the end of the scene, the mood is quickly charged with humor by the reappearance of the aunt, the uncle, and The Buyer.

An event that demonstrates for them that fantasy may become more real than reality is the arrival of Julia. Actually, she is Henrietta, a beauty-salon operator whom Beatriz had chanced to dial on the phone one day and who had accepted the role of silent confidant. When Henrietta-Julia announces that she knows the whereabouts of the real Eugene, The Buyer—who continues to enjoy every new happening and has neglected to go home—remarks significantly: "This is like the theater."

Henrietta brings Eugene, now sick and prematurely aged, to the apartment, but Beatriz pretends not to recognize him and leaves on the arm of Villalba. In her parting line she reveals her need for revenge for ten years of loneliness: "We're going before the stationery store closes. Eugene needs an eraser. . . . So I'll go with him. So he won't have a pretext for going off with another woman and leaving me alone for ten years. . . ."

After ten years without a husband, Beatriz now has two, and Carolina delivers another pointed comment on the similarity of affairs to the theater: "Our play was very well worked out but it's like the theater. When the author turns his back, the actors do what they please. . . ." Finally, Villalba concludes that his dream with Beatriz must end, that the presence of the real Eugene makes its continuation impossible. Then Beatriz deliberately returns to reality and explains to Eugene why she had chosen illusion rather than the truth of his desertion. In a powerful confrontation scene she lays bare all the truth behind her ten years of pretense and dismisses the unfaithful husband coldly and forever. Reluctantly he leaves, and Beatriz refuses to utter his name as she says good-bye. She turns to her aunt for a moment of comfort but is not long in taking steps to create a new life for herself through an ingenious manipulation of time. She telephones Julia, and during the conversation it becomes clear that she has put away the memory of her husband and will step back in time to the point just before she had met him. Then she calls Villalba, addressing him by his real name, to inform him that she will see him soon and that "Eugene has just died." The aunt and uncle listen with increasing satisfaction, and Gerard happily prepares his next newspaper advertisement. They are eager to return to illusion; but this illusion seems destined to provide the means for Beatriz's eventual marriage to Villalba and a new and more authentic life.

López Rubio has been praised repeatedly for his masterful use of language, and it is perhaps in *The Blindfold* that his versatility is most evident. The dialogue ranges from near-absurdist and near-farcical to poetically eloquent. There are subtle shifts from whimsical and even inconsequential, lines (which occasionally recall the theater of Jardiel Poncela) to passages which convey the underlying anguish of the protagonist. Amusing epigrams abound, and topical allusions are made with disregard for posterity. Carolina remarks on the arrival of Ava Gardner to Spain, and there are references to American aid, the Big Four, Metro-Goldwyn-Mayer (with a pun on the word "metro"), Josephine Baker, and the Castellana Hilton.

Above all, *The Blindfold* presents a magnificent and uninhibited theatricalization of life in which the humanity of the characters is preserved. In discussing Pirandello's *Six Characters in Search of an Author*, Francis Fergusson has written that the Italian playwright sees human life itself as theatrical. "He inverts the convention of modern realism; instead of pretending that the stage is not the stage at all, but the familiar parlor, he pretends that the familiar parlor is not real, but a stage, containing many 'realities'." [11] López Rubio has expressed his admiration for Pirandello, [12] and he shares with him the fundamental concept that life is in essence theatrical. Like the French dramatist Jean Anouilh and the contemporary Spanish writer Víctor Ruiz Iriarte, [13] López Rubio is strongly attracted to a type of theater-within-theater that is Pirandellian in inspiration, though not imitative in execution. This inspiration is unmistakable in *Alberto*, *Celos del aire*, and *The Blindfold*; but these plays also bear the particular stamp of their author in their dialogue, in the skillful balance between the comical and the serious, and in their ultimate rejection of pessimism.

II La otra orilla *(The Other Shore)*

In *The Other Shore*, López Rubio employed the supernatural for the first time in his second career. Not since *Overnight* had he dealt with a dramatic situation that transcended the known limits of human experience. The four principal characters are killed at the beginning of the play and appear only as ghosts who can discuss their predicament among themselves but cannot communicate with the several living characters in the play. After the first act, their "earthly remains" are removed and only their nonphysical beings are left. The work proved an exceptionally popular piece, and it was evident in the commentaries which appeared after the premiere that it had been recognized as being more than a clever comedy on a basically macabre theme. For example, Elías Gómez Picazo described the essence of the play in his review for the newspaper *Madrid*:

> The work is a meditation on the world from a place in which the world's passions lose their value and hypocrisy gives way to truth. For this reason, this work of López Rubio is not untranscendental, in spite of its humoristic wrapping and surface lightness. On the contrary, it constitutes a worthy lesson on the fiction and blindness that seem to surround and determine human actions and reactions. The love that is right beside us and we fail to recognize; the heroic posture of a vindication of honor that obeys motives that are much less noble; the faith we deposit on those who do not deserve it; the love we're sure of but which is really based on selfishness and convenience . . . form the analysis of life which this work realizes with exemplary skill and delicacy, to end on a note of hope, symbolized in that rebirth of illusion and love that frame the final passing of the two principal characters.[14]

It was, of course, noted that there were numerous theatrical antecedents for *The Other Shore*, plays in which the dead figured in the action in one manner or another. Enrique Sordo was reminded particularly of Sutton Vane,[15] and Marqueríe added a list of others ranging from Tirso de Molina to Molnar, while defending the originality of López Rubio's dramatic treatment.[16]

In the opening scene of *The Other Shore*, two of the principals, Leonardo and Ana, are enjoying an illicit evening in the house of Leonardo's aunt. They are shot by Ana's "wronged" husband (Jaime), who is in turn killed by the police. A fourth victim is Martín, who had been walking his dog at an inopportune time and happened to get in the way of Jaime's first shot. Death continues to be a great equalizer and also an eliminator of the passions; but in López Rubio's comedy, the dead characters retain for a short time an interest in the world they are leaving. The four spirits remain temporarily at the scene of their demise and are able to observe the reactions of their relatives and associates. All of the falseness and hypocrisy of their former existences is made vividly clear to them. And in the course of their own discussions, it is revealed that while each had been engaged in deception, he in turn had been the victim of a similar kind of deceit. All have engaged in fruitless and rather passionless sexual liaisons. Only after it is too late do they realize that they have never experienced genuine love.

But even in death, López Rubio's characters are capable of lies and self-delusion. Ana maintains to Jaime that her meeting with Leonardo had been quite innocent (even though his view through the window had indicated otherwise) and that she had come to the house to reclaim some compromising letters from a friend named Eugenia. Ironically, Leonardo did have some letters from Eugenia, and both Jaime and Martín had also been involved with her at one time or another.

The end of the first act is enlivened by the introduction of two policemen (Ibáñez 138 and Ibáñez 257) and Martín's superstitious housekeeper (Rufina).[17] Marqueríe calls them *"tipos sainetescos"* (characters using popular dialect and mannerisms of their class), which were frequently favored by Jardiel Poncela in his comedies and which are perfectly in keeping with the tragicomic tradition.[18] Rufina's humorous and straightforward attitude and speech contrast amusingly with the more sophisticated manner of the other female characters, while through the policemen a very inspired type of suspense is added to the play.

As in *The Blindfold*, the dialogue contains references to topical matters, such as Vietnam, German unity, the Voice of America, and Russia and her satellites. Another kind of humor is achieved when a character interrupts a serious conversation with an irrelevant question or statement—adding a touch of the absurd—as when Martín is describing his ill-fated outing with his dog:

MARTÍN.   (*Thinking back.*) I came over here. I told my dog to follow me. . . .
LEONARDO.   (*Interested in the dog*) What breed is he?
MARTÍN.   Scottish Terrier.
LEONARDO.   What color?
MARTÍN.   Black, with a few white spots. . . . Do you like dogs too?
LEONARDO. (*Excited.*) Very much. I have a. . . .[19]

The playwright also shows us the humor in the "rituals" of infidelity, which has its special conventions; but beneath the humor is an almost sad irony. Perhaps the most telling irony is in the dialogue in which the dead characters resort to the clichés involving death from force of habit, even though they have meaning only from the point of view of the living.

In the second act of *The Other Shore*, Martín's selfish nephew (Diego), Leonardo's wife (Carlota), and his sister-in-law (Felisa) arrive to examine the scene of the crime. Diego makes no effort to hide his pleasure at becoming his uncle's heir. Already he had engaged in an attempt to take over Martín's interests and had coerced a basically loyal but underpaid lawyer (Roca) who directs Martín's business affairs. The only person among the survivors who really felt love for any of the deceased is Felisa, Leonardo's sister-in-law, and she alone is able to see the four ghosts. But her sorrow has not dulled her feminine awareness, nor does the shock of seeing Ana's ghost prevent her from noticing the stylish dress she is wearing.

Carlota has brought along her young paramour (Mauricio) who finds her less interesting now that her husband is dead and she is showing an unmistakable inclination toward remarriage. When Mauricio walks out on Carlota, both Jaime and Martín express some pity for the widow; however, Ana is more realistic:

JAIME. Poor woman!
MARTÍN. Yes. She's just missed the last train.
ANA. Don't worry. She has a car.

The spirits are indignant at the behavior of the survivors but they are helpless to protest. The second act ends with the startling news that one of the four "dead" characters is really only in a coma. This is disclosed through a telephone call to Ibáñez 138.[20] But the audience is left in suspense because the policeman has forgotten to ask which body is alive; and when he attempts to call back, the line is busy. Now the question that preoccupies the four ghosts is the identity of the survivor. They discuss the failures of their former existences. Only Martín shows less than utter distaste for life—and even he would not wish to return with the memory of this intermediary state. Leonardo denounces the world of business that he had known in life, and its double standard of morality:

LEONARDO. Business men have their own natural immorality, but they're implacable when it comes to other kinds of immorality. . . . My buildings could break apart and collapse, and my name would remain untarnished as there had been benefits for everyone concerned—except, of course, the victims. And my romantic involvements would be tolerated as long as they could be talked about in whispers, with a smile. But an open scandal upsets wives. . . .

Through gradual elimination, it becomes apparent which of the characters are really dead, for they begin to disappear through the French windows of the living room: first Jaime, and then Leonardo. When Martín and Ana are left alone, Martín tells Ana that he loves her, in spite of her defects. There is an undeniable attraction in the woman's basic femininity. If she lacks faith, and cannot even commit her sins with conviction, she is, nevertheless, only a product of the age in which she happened to be born:

MARTÍN.   You're not to blame. You're a product of the time in which we live, without faith in anything—or with excessive, unreasoning faith in something. Of a world that is trying to exhaust every sensation as quickly as possible, because it forsees its own atomic disintegration. Even those it's not interested in. . . . You are a model of our age.

Now Ana, too, begins to disappear, and Martín calls after her in desperation, believing that he is destined to remain behind alone. The telephone rings, and Ibáñez 138 receives the news that the surviving victim has died. The audience knows that it was Martín, who follows Ana, calling her name. But the two policemen never learn the identity of the victim who had clung to life a few hours nor the lesson of those few hours.

   In *The Other Shore*, López Rubio demonstrates more clearly than in any previous work his awareness of the moral ambivalence of contemporary man, and he expresses in the play his observations on the lack of values in both private and public life. Jaime enacts the role of the wronged husband, but he lacks the convictions of honor of the Calderonian world; his real concern is "what people will say." Even the loyal business servant, Señor Roca, is drawn toward secret crime (what is currently known as "white-collar crime") to satisfy material dreams that are in themselves rather pathetic. The dramatist does not condemn these people, at least not Ana, who, in spite of her lack of genuine passion, retains something of the eternal feminine—a virtue in itself, in the opinion of the playwright, and a redeeming quality. López Rubio observes but does not lecture. He gives no direct answers, but suggests that, on an individual plane, the beginning of redemption may be in a love that is not based on self-interest.

   When he presented *The Other Shore*, López Rubio risked comparison of the play with both Jardiel Poncela's *Un marido de ida y vuelta* (A Round-Trip Husband) and Noel Coward's *Blithe Spirit*, in which the dead return to influence the actions of the living in similar ways, leading to comparable comic-macabre endings. But by requiring the audience to relate to the action onstage from the point of view of the dead characters from the very beginning rather than to the "reality" of the living, he created a work that was quite dissimilar from the earlier comedies of Jardiel and Coward.[21] In addition, the dead characters onstage and the audience in the theater are equally affected by the suspense introduced at the end of the second act; consequently, actors become audience and, in a sense, the audience becomes a part of the play.

The Other Shore differs from López Rubio's earlier major comedies in a fundamental aspect: the characters themselves do not participate in a deliberate theatricalization of life, even though they betray at times an awareness of their own theatricalness in their words or actions. While pretence is unmasked and "truth" contrasted with supposed reality, illusion is never sought or transformed into a new reality. Consequently, the play represents a turning away from the more apparent Pirandellian techniques that had characterized López Rubio's most important efforts from *Alberto* through *The Blindfold*.

CHAPTER 6

Other Plays of Mid-Career

I Cuenta nueva (*A New Account*)

O N September 30, 1954, López Rubio had his first premiere in Barcelona with *A New Account*, a basically serious play about two generations of a Catalán business family. It was not received with much favor by the critics and although it was later performed in other Spanish cities, it was never seen in Madrid. Enrique Sordo, in a review for the magazine *Revista*, found *A New Account* uninteresting and old-fashioned for the most part, and its performance dull—although he did admit to liking certain individual scenes which involved the character known as "La Madre" (The Mother). [1] Julio Coll, whose hostility toward López Rubio's theater had been demonstrated on more than one occasion, quoted comments made by the playwright to a newspaper interviewer the day before the premiere. With typical frankness, López Rubio had evaluated (and perhaps underestimated) his own talent as a dramatist, describing himself as "a facile writer, ingenious, light, who prefers to play [jugar] with small, human problems . . . who walks a narrow line which has, on one side, humor, and on the other side, poetry; whose dialogue is better than his construction; who attempts to draw a smile from the audience and proposes a game in which he wants the audience to collaborate." [2] Coll applauded the playwright's candid self-evaluation and defining of his dramatic boundaries. However, it is impossible not to suspect that López Rubio had calculated his remarks to disarm critics who had ignored the aesthetic merits of his plays or categorically dismissed them because they lacked a specific political or social message.

Despite some obvious flaws in construction and realization, *A New Account* is not without dramatic interest. It is set in the office of a Barcelona textile factory rather than the customary sitting-room of a number of López Rubio's works of this period. While the characters tend to resemble those from earlier plays in their facility of speech, their motivations are more complex, and they are developed with considerable psychological insight. As in *Twenty and Forty*, a serious marital problem is resolved in a hopeful manner, even though a somber or unhappy ending might seem equally possible, and the play ends with a scene of mutual understanding that promises a successful relationship in the future.

In form, *A New Account* is the most loosely-structured of López Rubio's plays of mid-career, and the events of the five scenes take place over a period of more than a year. Although the playwright had shown his mastery of the one-set play, there are entrances or exits in *A New Account* that seem contrived to bring about a key confrontation between two characters. Clearly, a setting which would have permitted encounters outside the office would have given the play a more natural flow of action.

The first act is dominated by the seventy-year-old "Madre," who has spent thirty years of her life directing the textile business inherited from her husband and who is now approaching death. Her sole heir, a rather weak and ineffectual young man (Jorge), seems incapable of carrying on after his mother dies. She is sensitive to her son's limitations and is not unaware of the reasons for them. He has not even inherited his father's defects: he is "too good, too submissive, too accustomed to his mother's protection." [3] Like many of López Rubio's women characters, the Mother speaks knowingly of marital problems, for she has had to achieve a modus vivendi with her husband's infidelity. She reminisces without bitterness and clings to the past, looking upon contemporary ways with as much distaste as the Marquesa in *Alberto*:

THE MOTHER. Today diplomacy talks of balances, of clearings, of credits and of compensations. The only treaties that are occasionally honored are business treaties. And there's more espionage in factories and laboratories than in military installations and chancelleries.

Recognizing the strong character of the daughter (Nuria) of her chief overseer (Don Germán), she entrusts the future of her business to the girl and persuades her to marry Jorge. The only threat to the old woman's plan is the presence of Ramón Valls, a young worker who is in love with Nuria. When Ramón leaves for America, the Mother pays him two years' salary instead of the three months' pay suggested by Don Germán. As the old woman says, "It's not too much to raise up a bridge of silver."

In the second act, Nuria continues the "cuenta vieja," the old ways established by the Mother. Dressed in dark mourning clothes and seated in the office chair, she is almost indistinguishable from her late predecessor. Although she is now married to Jorge, their marital relationship is sexually lukewarm, and Nuria is little more than a mother substitute. The old woman remains the real protagonist of the play even in death, for the wife is merely fulfilling her role, both in the business and in the care of the son. Even Nuria's gestures, and the caresses she gives Jorge, are like those of the Mother.

Two new characters are introduced in the second act. The first is a pretty and rather impertinent secretary (Montserrat or "Monse") who attracts Jorge and becomes the "other woman." The second is Nuria's mother (Mercedes), who had been mentioned earlier as a seriously ill woman under the care of her faithful and attentive daughter. Thanks to the expensive medical attention she has received since Nuria's marriage, Mercedes is not only well but vigorous. Don Germán remarks that she is now "estrenando salud, estrenando voz, y estrenando autoridad" (that is, showing off her health, showing off her voice, and throwing her weight around). A highly amusing but somewhat exaggerated creation, she supplies comic relief; however, a character portrayed with less vivid strokes might have been more appropriate to the tone of the play.

Jorge is drawn to Monse and begins to acquire the masculine assuredness that he had previously lacked; then Ramón returns to offer Nuria a "complete" love. He represents the antithesis of the man whom Nuria has married, the man who sees her as the mother of his children. But the love he offers excludes the element of illusion that López Rubio finds essential to enduring, emotionally creative relationships. When Nuria discovers that Jorge is taking Monse with him to a business convention in Barcelona, she experiences a moment of truth and decides to fight for her husband's love. She orders the dead mother's chair and embroidery frame removed from the office—a symbolical gesture which exorcises the lingering influence of the past.

In the final act, new furnishings have replaced the old pieces that had belonged to the Mother, and Nuria appears transformed in new, attractive clothes. Mercedes is on hand to advise, but her daughter tells her: "Look, Mama, if you've come in the mood to see a drama,

you've come to the wrong street. The cinema is one block up."
Mercedes's retort is a typical López Rubio jibe at the censorship of
motion pictures:

MERCEDES.   Really, daughter! Films dealing with these matters are
always cut. Or they change the plot in the dubbing. They turn the other
woman into the husband's aunt, and a virtuous one at that. And don't tell me
there's anything interesting about that. Real life is much more entertaining.[4]

Ramón still hopes to overcome Nuria's loyalty to Jorge and to
persuade her to go away with him, but she dismisses him with
confidence in her new view of life: "The past is dead. From this day on
it's a new account. . . . I only needed an eraser to finish off the old
one." Ramón warns Nuria that Jorge will never live up to her ideals,
but she remains firm. Jorge returns from Barcelona with an enthusiasm for business (as well as for his masculine role). Nuria welcomes
his new aggressiveness and wins him back from Monse by asserting
herself in a genuinely feminine way. There is no real assurance at the
end of the play that Jorge's affair is over or that other women won't
come along to attract him, perhaps with fewer scruples than the
secretary; but Nuria has successfully demonstrated her own sexual
powers.

López Rubio delineates, step by step, the building of the sexual
illusion, suggesting that love thrives on novelty (supplied by the
ingenuity and calculation of the lover) as well as on the natural
impetus of desire. For both Nuria and Jorge, it is necessary to
undergo a psychological change—essentially stepping out of the
shadow of the Mother (who had demanded adherence to the "script"
even in death) and becoming themselves. Only then is a deep and
passionate involvement possible for them.

A New Account is obviously not without its moments of dramatic
force and psychological insight; but it lacks the sheer theatricalism,
the blend of irony and poetry, that characterize the serious comedies
of this period of the playwright's career. The humor that does occur in
the work seems grafted onto a serious play rather than an integral part
of the dramatic fabric.

II   El caballero de Barajas
(The Gentleman from Barajas)

Directed by López Rubio himself, *The Gentleman from Barajas*
was first performed on September 23, 1955, at the large Teatro

Alcázar. The Premio María Rolland for 1955 was awarded to the playwright and to the composer, Manuel Parada, for this musical comedy, and the popular singing artist Luis Sagi-Vela received an award for his interpretation of the role of Fernando.

Both lyrics and dialogue contain some amusing commentary on contemporary Madrid, but the plot itself is based on a fantastic idea: The transfer of a voice from one person to another.[5] Indalecio, a comic pseudoscientist, presents an invention which enables the valet (Fernando) of an aging and very conceited opera singer (Fabiani) to use his employer's golden voice when the singer is asleep. Within two months he becomes a popular singing star. There is, expectedly, an attractive ingenue (Rosita) who falls in love with Fernando, and the "other woman," an Argentine actress who has had thirteen husbands and who dismisses her current lover (a Polish poet) in favor of Fernando. There are complications when the voice of the great Fabiani is "lost." However, it is soon recovered, and, through the generosity of the opera singer, Fernando has the use of the voice for his career.

For all the absurdities of the plot, there are sections of *The Gentleman from Barajas* which are amusingly satirical. A prime example is the scene in which Indalecio recounts to Fernando the opportunities that his new fame has brought him to endorse products and to appear in a new motion picture process called "panoramascope," which has a screen so wide that the actors have to perform all their scenes lying down. And in the lyrics of the songs there are humorous topical references. One song, "The Gentleman from Barajas," explains the title of the work, describing the influx of American actresses to Spain and the "gentlemen" who wait at the Barajas airport to see that they don't remain unescorted. Another song, sung by Indalecio, predicts how the "old" Madrid will be lamented in the year 2000. There are, on the other hand, sentimental and romantic songs with titles such as "La luna sale para todos" (The Moon Comes Out for Everyone), "Te quiero sólo a ti" (I Love Only You), and "Canción a medianoche" (Song at Midnight), which express the conventional sentiments expected of such compositions.

Although the basic elements of *The Gentleman from Barajas*—dialogue, song, and dance—are to be found in the traditional Spanish *zarzuela* and in the popular musical reviews of Madrid, the book and lyrics indicate that López Rubio was attempting a more timely and sophisticated type of lyric theater resembling the American musical comedy (a theatrical genre that has had only limited success with Spanish audiences).

III   La novia del espacio
(The Love from Space)

The Love from Space, a play in which comedy and serious poetic drama were combined, had its first performance in Barcelona on February 16, 1956, and proved to be the most complete failure of López Rubio's career. The plot of the work centered on an encounter between an extraterrestrial being and a girl in rural Spain. In the months prior to the production of the play there had been considerable publicity and speculation on flying saucers in the Spanish press, but this seems not to have created much interest in audiences for "science-fiction" theater. In spite of the acknowledged excellence of the acting and staging, *The Love from Space* was not successful.

In the magazine *Revista*, Enrique Sordo described the dramatic situation in some detail and concluded that it was a total miscalculation on López Rubio's part:

In *The Love from Space*, José López Rubio presents us, under a good "science fiction" title, the story of a girl from the provinces, a self-styled descendent of Don Quixote, who falls in love and commits a pecadillo with a handsome interstellar man, who has descended in a flying saucer to La Mancha, no less. As can be seen, it deals with an interesting matter—not very original, but full of possibilities that could have been developed in two directions: 1. creating a climate of poetic mystery, as the author has done on other occasions, and 2. taking advantage of the multitude of amusing situations that can easily be derived from this basic plot. But it is clear that López Rubio has wanted both orientations, the grotesque and the poetic, and the result has been that one has cancelled out the other. . . . Not a single situation appears throughout *The Love from Space* that succeeds in amusing or impressing. But let us note two moments of quality that are superior to the rest of the piece: the father's confession, which concludes the second act, and the tender declaration of "Juan Simple" to the protagonist. Where the gratuitousness and inconsistency of the play reach their limit is in the absurd and very poor final resolution in which an invisible, but audible, flying saucer comes in search of the deceived girl. This naive conclusion, which doubtless was not very well thought out, is the colophon of this work which has disappointed so much and which lacks the habitual dramatic mastery of its author. . . .[6]

Actually, Sordo was more precise and to the point in criticizing *The Love from Space* than was frequently the case with Spanish drama critics: he specified what he liked and disliked and indicated why. But his critique leaves the contemporary reader with the suspicion that

the play was written and staged at the wrong time, and that its
dramatic values may be greater than was recognized in 1956. It is
possible that López Rubio's fantastic and poetic ending for the work
might seem more effective to a generation that responded so warmly
to *Close Encounters of the Third Kind.*[7] López Rubio himself was not
satisfied with *The Love from Space* in its original form, and he gave
some thought to rewriting the play. However, the script remains
unpublished, and a new version was never attempted.[8]

IV   Un trono para Cristy *(A Throne for Cristy)*

After his venture into musical comedy in 1955 and the unsuccessful
production of *The Love from Space* in Barcelona in 1956, López
Rubio wrote a somewhat more typical play with an overall satirical
point of view but with pronounced sentimental touches. First performed on September 14, 1956, *A Throne for Cristy* did not prove to
be one of his more successful productions in spite of a cast which
included such outstanding performers as Isabel Garcés, Julia Gutiérrez Caba, and Irene Caba Alba. In Madrid, the critical reception was
polite but hardly enthusiastic. While pointing out that the theme of
the comedy was not at all original, Marqueríe found attractive qualities in López Rubio's treatment of the situation and considered the
elements of the comedy tasteful and well balanced.[9] Alfonso Sánchez
described the play as an entertaining piece of theater.[10] But after the
opening in Barcelona in October 1957, Enrique Sordo wrote a particularly negative critique of the play in which he declared that brilliant
dialogue was not sufficient justification for a theatrical production.[11]
    The action of *A Throne for Cristy* takes place in a cottage on
Mallorca (an island favored by international tourists) and is concerned
with the efforts of a penniless American woman (Pamela) to achieve
royal status for her daughter (Cristy). In her uninhibited exercise of a
fertile imagination, Pamela is not unlike several of the women in
other plays of López Rubio. She has lost her husband, a German
mechanic who returned to Europe during World War II, and is
presently surviving through her skill in putting off her creditors with
fictions. When a local merchant (Señor Pascual) arrives to present his
bill, Pamela begins to talk amusingly of her cattle (nonexistent)
somewhere in Kansas. But the moment that Señor Pascual leaves,
Pamela reveals the desperation that she has been hiding beneath all
her lively words. She sits down dejectedly and takes a handful of
unpaid bills from a box, exclaiming: "My God! My God! My God!"[12]

At the entrance of Cristy, an attractive teenage girl, the mother resumes her pretense of gaiety. By chance, a middle-aged foreign couple arrive to look at the cottage—which the landlord hopes to rent if he can remove the present occupants—and Pamela arranges for them to overhear her say that Cristy is a princess. She pledges the tourists to secrecy, knowing full well that they will disclose this fascinating piece of news at the earliest opportunity. With the unwitting help of the foreign couple, and the eager cooperation of an aspiring young journalist, the story that Cristy is heiress to the throne of Kapf-Leidenstein quickly spreads beyond the shores of Mallorca.

Much of the humor in *A Throne for Cristy* derives from the colorful secondary characters and their pert dialogue, particularly Doña Reme, an elderly woman who "serves for everything and lives off that specialization." Reme sees through Pamela's fantasies, and she criticizes the mother for pampering Cristy; but when it becomes evident that the girl will actually be accepted as the legal princess, Reme joins the intrigue with enthusiasm. Another amusing female character is Milagros, a florist who also begins to appreciate the value of her association with a "royal family."

Attracted by the widespread publicity, the vice-president of the "Society for the Restoration of European Thrones," (Du Vanel) appears to lend his services to the American pretender. Shortly afterwards, the Grand Duchess Clara Augusta, a great-aunt of the princess, arrives "incognito" to look over the situation for herself. She is a humorous specimen of royalty, with a touch of British eccentricity. She explains to Pamela her particular relationship to the father of the princess, how she had pampered him and allowed him the pleasures his straitlaced mother had forbidden. She ends her long speech with a pointed and pertinent question: "Does he still like raspberry tarts?"

Since Pamela's "lost" husband had been a European, had possessed mechanical talents that the Grand Duchess had happened to mention, and had liked raspberries, there is now the possibility that the illusion which she deliberately created may turn out to be reality. However, at this moment, the audience is more convinced of this possibility than Pamela. Then in a recognition scene that is more whimsical than dramatic, the Grand Duchess accepts Cristy as the genuine princess.

A new note of seriousness comes into the play in the third act when Pamela realizes that she must give up her close personal relationship with her daughter now that the girl has acquired the status of royalty:

CRISTY. Mama. . . .
PAMELA. Yes, my child. . . .
CRISTY. (*Indicating Du Vanel with a gesture*.) We have been thinking. . . .
PAMELA. What?
CRISTY. It would be better if you didn't come to the airport. . . .
PAMELA. (*She hesitates, without knowing what to answer*.) Ah! (*Finding a justification*.) But if nobody goes! . . .
CRISTY. There'll be someone there, in any event. . . . People from the consulate . . . and perhaps some dignitary. You'd become emotional. I know you. A scene, before people, would be ridiculous. . . . We have to get used to controlling our emotions. . . .
PAMELA. (*Resigned*.) As you wish. . . .

Doña Reme urges Pamela to tell Cristy the "truth" before it is too late, but the mother refuses. Unexpectedly, Pamela's husband (Hans) appears. After Cristy has departed, her father reveals that he really is a prince but that he doesn't want the job. He and Pamela will return to America together, but now a new story will have to be invented to explain the presence of a strange man. The play ends with the suggestion that Pamela's capacity for fantasy has not been diminished by the rapid changes in her life: "Everyone knows me now. . . . I can no longer live with a man, without an explanation. . . . I'll have to invent something. . . . Wait . . . I have it! . . . We can say that. . . ." And for a moment Pamela recalls the more desperate Gloria Velarde of *Remedy in Memory* (on a lighter level, to be sure).

Although there are moments of seriousness in *A Throne for Cristy*, the play remains lighter in substance than López Rubio's major serious comedies. As critics noted, the theme of the work is a familiar one which has served as a basis for varied types of theater. As popular entertainment, the play serves its purpose well; its dialogue has an expected appeal, and it offers as well some effective satire on the habits of international tourists and the behavior of native Europeans in the face of the postwar invasion. López Rubio may have attempted a more bitingly satirical play than he actually achieved. Even though the pretentions of a sector of society are seen in an absurd light, the sentimental elements tend too often to overshadow and negate the effect the playwright probably had in mind.

V   Las manos son inocentes
(Our Hands Are Innocent)

Before the premiere of *Our Hands Are Innocent*, on October 2, 1958, it might reasonably have been concluded that López Rubio would continue to find his most satisfactory expression in the area of intellectual comedy and poetic fantasy, and that serious drama devoid of humor would remain outside his realm of creative interest. However, this stark and uncompromising exploration of human guilt and remorse revealed a new aspect of the playwright's art and marked the most significant advance in his career since his return to the theater in 1949. No doubt *Our Hands are Innocent* came as a surprise to López Rubio's critics and as a revelation to the thoughtful elements of his public. It is evident from the playwright's *autocrítica* that he attended the first performance of his new play with some trepidation. Aware of his reputation as a writer of comedies—both serious and light—which had grown over a period of nine years, he recognized the possibility that an atypical work of such somber content, no matter how skillfully written, might well be received unfavorably:

I have felt the desire to seek, far from my customary means, other dramatic spaces. I have attempted to test myself in other ambitions for which I find myself inexpert, as defenseless as the day, now almost thirty years in the past, of my first battle. With the timidity of a new author, with uncertainty—and why not?—with much curiosity about myself, I approach tonight the illustrious stage of the María Guerrero, ready, at the slightest indication, to return to my simple shoes.[13]

The first performance of the new work was warmly received by the audience, which "listened with great attention and applauded insistently at the ends of both acts, demanding at both times the presence of the author."[14] But the critical reception, while generally favorable, was qualified in several instances. Eusebio García Luengo, commenting subjectively on the acclaim extended to the play by the audience, observed: "As for the reaction of the audience the night of the premiere, it is probable that it felt moved by that drama or that, on the contrary, it was in the mood for a dialectic, cold, and cerebral game of the type to which the French are so addicted."[15] Sergio Nerva, an admirer of López Rubio's theater, praised the literary and dramatic talents revealed in the drama.[16] Later, in his introduction to the annual *Teatro español*, Sainz de Robles declared that this was "a perfect work, amazingly perfect."[17] When *Our Hands Are Innocent* was performed in Barcelona in 1959, Enrique Sordo criticized what he considered an excessive use of elements of suspense and a non-realistic, literary language, but he admitted that it was a "play not to be disdained."[18] The critics seemed bent on finding literary antecedents and possible influences, and the names of Ugo Betti, Graham Greene, Faulkner, and even Benavente appeared in their commentaries.

Actually, López Rubio found inspiration for the title of his play in a passage from Racine's *Phèdre* (Act I, Scene 3), which also states the theme of the contemporary work:

> Grâces au Ciel, mes mains ne sont point
> criminelles. . . .
> Plût aux Dieux que mon coeur fût innocent
> comme elles!

This quotation prefaces the published text of *Our Hands Are Innocent*, and it suggests that the playwright was attempting a drama along classical lines. The application of the traditional unities was noted by Marquerie,[19] and Juan Emilio Aragonés saw a secondary character ("la Portera" or "Concierge") in a role representing that of the chorus;[20] but the other possible associations with Greek tragedy were not explored.

The event around which the entire play centers takes place prior to the opening scene. It is the death of the Boarder (Señor Guevara) who had been living in a rented room in the shabby apartment of Germán and Paula, a middle-aged couple. Germán is an unsuccessful writer whose spirit has been eroded by continual failure to find identity and professional recognition in society. His office job has only added to his frustration. Beset by pressing financial problems, the couple is tempted by the money which Guevara has in his possession and plots to kill him. The inner action of the two acts develops from a series of revelations concerning the true cause of death.

The curtain rises on a shadowy room furnished in well-worn and outmoded pieces. As the stage directions indicate, the setting reflects the couple's moral and spiritual decay and defines their economic situation.[21] It is three o'clock in the morning, and Germán and Paula are returning from the emergency room where the invalid boarder has just died of a sudden attack. The couple assumes that he has succumbed to a poison which Paula had substituted for his customary medication. From the moment of their return to the apartment, they are troubled by the memory of their act, and their growing remorse and sense of guilt, affected by certain revelations, provide the substance of their "debate." The initial exchange is interrupted by the appearance of the Portera, an outspoken and inquisitive popular type who comments on the action of the drama. She describes the personality and behavior of the dead man and provides a contrast to the somber introspection of the principals. Through her words the dead Boarder acquires an identity for the audience.

When Germán goes to Guevara's room to get his personal effects, the light that he turns on appears more brilliant than the one which illuminates the main setting, and provides a visual contrast. The stage directions give specific instructions concerning the several occasions when lights are turned off and on by the characters. In part, the actions reflect their habitual need to save money, but there is also a symbolical meaning to the play of light and darkness. The scenic elements complement and imitate the inner action of the drama. In this case, the physical action represents the passing from ignorance (both of self and of the true cause of the Boarder's death) to realization.

The symbolic use of the imagery of light and darkness is also to be found in the dialogue of *Our Hands Are Innocent*. The room of the deceased proves a source of revelation, and it is the scene of the crime which Paula cannot purge from her memory. Germán, returning to the dining room with a box full of documents, fails to extinguish the light, and Paula reminds him—indicating her desire to evade the reality of her deed:

PAULA. (*In a low voice*) Germán. . . . That light. . . .
GERMÁN. (*Knowing that Paula is thinking of something else.*) Haven't you finished with economizing yet?
PAULA. (*Avoiding Germán's look.*) It's not that.
GERMÁN. (*Who doesn't take his eyes off Paula.*) Put it out. (*Paula stands motionless, with her eyes down. Germán looks at her an instant, waiting. He has an expression of condescension, with a sense of irony. He goes to the hallway, puts out the light in the bedroom and closes the door. He returns to the dining room. Looking at Paula.*) It's done. It wasn't so difficult.

Among the papers, the couple discovers the name of a certain Señor Ramos who is the administrator of Guevara's affairs. Germán makes a telephone call to inform him of the death; meanwhile, Paula has recalled that Guevara had been writing when she entered his room with the poison and had thrown some papers into the wastebasket. Examining the contents, she discovers the two tablets of poison which she thought the Boarder had swallowed. This is the first of the revelation scenes providing a reversal of situation—in this instance, disclosing the fact that Paula and Germán have not actually committed a crime.[22] But the burden of guilt has not been removed.

Following the discovery of the poison, there is a telephone call (a modern device that is a convenient substitute for the messenger in Greek drama) informing the couple that there is some question about the real cause of Guevara's death and that an autopsy is to be per-

formed. Now they are faced with the ironic possibility that they may
be accused of a crime of which they are technically innocent. Señor
Ramos arrives and supplies information on the dead man's background. A further irony: Guevara had praised Germán and Paula to
Ramos for their *desinterés* (selflessness). The first act ends as the
lawyer begins to read the Boarder's final will.

The reading of the will continues in the second act. Guevara has left
all that he owned to the couple that attempted to murder him. It is
evident that he had overheard them discussing their financial problems; it is also possible that he was aware that they had discussed his
death. Suspicious of human motives, Germán concludes that the will
had been an intentional, devilish design to let them go the gallows
with all of their material needs satisfied. A new reversal of events
occurs with the arrival of a police agent (another version of the
classical messenger) who states that Guevara has left a suicide note
indicating that no one should be blamed for his death. The final
reversal of the situation results from a telephone call which
announces the report of the autopsy: death from natural causes.
Among the Boarder's personal effects Paula discovers an untouched
tube of poison tablets. Undoubtedly, Guevara had planned suicide
but had died before taking the poison. The Portera, who has been
present during the telephone conversation, takes the final announce-
ment as an end to the uncertainty and turmoil. Unaware of the impact
that the call has had on Germán and Paula, she asks a question which
stands out in her flow of words: "Don't you believe that God knows
what he has between his hands, and is always the watchful one, even
though it may seem that he's absentminded?"

A new character is introduced briefly in the final minutes of the
play. She is a young neighbor who has not been informed of Guevara's
death. When she inquires about his health, Paula conceals the truth
and tells her that the Boarder is better. For a moment, she has tried to
believe that the deed was never contemplated and that Guevara
could be still alive in the next room. But now the husband and wife
must endure together their remorse and the harsh truth of their
shared guilt. Again the playwright employs the imagery of light and
darkness. Paula tells Germán: "You have to lead me by the hand. I'm
blind . . . and you are beginning to see." Figuratively speaking,
Paula is—like Oedipus—blind, and she looks to Germán, who has
found the beginning of understanding (light) to be her guide. She
would like to go far away to find redemption, but her husband insists
that they stay in the apartment and that the inheritance remain

untouched. At Paula's request, Germán extinguishes the last artificial light, for the "brighter, cold light of day" is beginning to illuminate the room.

A parallel between Germán and Paula and Shakespeare's Macbeth and Lady Macbeth is apparent. Citing a review by Fernando Asís, José Castellano rejects the suggestion that the "innocent hands" of López Rubio's Paula are, in a sense, the reverse of the "bloodstained hands" of Lady Macbeth which ". . . provoke the confrontation of the character herself and her conscience, and with the consequences of the 'deed' that they originated." [23] Castellano maintains that Paula's incomplete crime is only a "state of conscience" which cannot have consequences beyond the individuals involved, but Lady Macbeth's completed crime "touches not only her—and her husband—but an entire society in which life must be respected." It is, however, debatable that the "incomplete" crime of Germán and Paula does not have a particular relevancy to the contemporary social structure in which they live. They are products of their society and reflect its faults. Macbeth and Lady Macbeth commit a violent and bloody murder to gain political power and its concomitant rewards. López Rubio's characters—in a more civilized age—plot their crime (a death they hope will appear to be natural and unmarked by exterior violence) because of their failure. They are brought to the point of murder more by an incapacity for finding fulfillment in modern society than by a passion for wealth or power. After all, as far as they knew, the money obtained through the death of Guevara would have given them only temporary relief at best. Both Lady Macbeth and her husband find death in a manner that is in keeping with the hideousness of their crime; the punishment of Paula and Germán—remorse and torture by conscience—is as outwardly invisible as their uncompleted murder.

Perhaps López Rubio's characters would have acquired greater dramatic stature if the playwright had chosen to write a prologue or a first act in which the couple could have been seen before the crime, as is the case in *Macbeth*. Shakespeare's characters consider their crime onstage before they commit it offstage. But it is clear that the author was interested in writing a drama along more economical lines, perhaps partly in consideration of the limited performance time in the Madrid theaters. If we consider his play to have a beginning, a middle, and an end, as Aristotle specifies, then the beginning must be the guilt of Paula and Germán; the middle is the reversal of the situation by the revelation of Guevara's compassion for his would-be murderers, leading to pathos; and the end is the self-realization which may lead to expiation.

Our Hands Are Innocent is a modern work constructed essentially on the pattern of classic tragedy. The unities are carefully observed; the chorus appears in the person of the Portera; and the modern invention, the telephone, on occasion serves as the "messenger." The dramatic tension is achieved through the reversal of the situation and revelations progressing through three stages. López Rubio was aware, of course, that his characters are no more like the traditional subjects of high tragedy than those of Arthur Miller's plays (two of which López Rubio had successfully adapted for the Spanish stage). Significantly, the author does not call his play a tragedy, but rather a *comedia dramática*. Following his own theatrical instincts, he applied those rules of classic drama that he found suitable for his own terse, intellectually slanted consideration of remorse and guilt.

CHAPTER 7

The Later Plays

I Diana está comunicando
(Diana's Mind Is Busy)

IN 1960, after having displayed a new aspect of his dramatic talents
in *Our Hands Are Innocent*, López Rubio turned again to comedy
and created a blithe and sophisticated work entitled *Diana's Mind Is
Busy*. Commenting on his selection of the play for inclusion in *Teatro
español, 1959–60*, Sainz de Robles wrote:

Everything about this comedy is enchanting: the theme, the episodes, the
dialogue, the wit and humor, the poetry of the majority of the lines, the
nature of the characters. It hardly seems necessary to mention its literary
quality and style, when it is so well known that López Rubio is a playwright
with a command of the most terse, the richest, and the most flavorful
language; and of a technique carried to the limits of its generic possibilities.[1]

Granted that Sainz de Robles's admiration may be somewhat overstated, his estimation of the play is not an unreasonable one—if it is
kept in mind that the playwright intended to create nothing more
than a well-written and original theatrical diversion with the measured theatrical effects that he understood so well. *Diana's Mind Is
Busy* does not offer the subtle blend of humor, irony, and poetic
reality that is associated with *Celos del aire* or *The Blindfold*, but it is
an intelligent comedy with some of the most amusing scenes that
López Rubio has written for the stage. The title role, originally
conceived for and performed by Conchita Montes, affords splendid
opportunities for the display of comic talents; and the secondary
female part, while briefer, is only slightly less rewarding to the
performer.

Diana, the protagonist of the play, is a mental telepathist, a "receiver" at first, and later an exceedingly successful "sender." She

101

appears unexpectedly in the office of Gonzalo, a psychiatrist who has been experimenting with telepathy and who has just lost the services of a "receiver" named Helenio. Diana is a celebrity of the moment who is performing with her partner (Eddy) in a Madrid variety theater. Her actual entrance does not occur until near the end of the first act, but the preliminary scenes are enlivened by the exchanges of dialogue between Gonzalo's nurse (Paulina) and Helenio, and by the appearance of an eccentric woman who continues to come to the office for imaginary appointments, even though she has been discharged.

When she enters the doctor's waiting room, Diana knows only that she has received a "summons". In dialogue liberally sprinkled with phrases and exclamations from some of the fourteen languages she speaks, she asks where she is and reveals her "supersensitive" status by detecting an autograph book in the desk drawer of the nurse. Gonzalo enters and immediately notes the attractiveness of the young telepathist. He explains his own scientific interests, and Diana realizes that the summons had really come from the doctor. After an appointment is arranged for the following day, Diana receives a "call" from Eddy and leaves for the theater.

The second act takes place in Gonzalo's private apartment. Diana returns for her appointment and has her first encounter with the doctor's fiancée (Florita), whose appearance and personality are satirically described by the playwright in the stage directions:

> She is young and very cute. Brought up in a school taught by nuns in the bosom of a respectable and well-to-do family. She smiles almost constantly and adopts a tone of prefabricated sweetness, even when she is saying the most terrible things, with the worst intentions, without losing her calculated air of naiveté for a moment. She is the perfect girl to bring happiness to a man who likes that kind of happiness. Her family and her intimate friends call her a jewel. In short, she resembles a female TV commentator.[2]

Florita is a recognizable contemporary Spanish type, and one which the dramatist intends to present in a devastatingly satirical manner. There is little doubt as to which woman will ultimately marry Gonzalo after Diana resolves to win the *"guerra fría"* (cold war). However, since the pretty telepathist is a receiver, the doctor is able to control her words and prevents her from obeying her feminine instincts in her first conversation with Florita. She finds herself treating the girl with utmost affection, and Florita is charmed. When she is able to escape from the doctor's influence for a moment, Diana expresses her feelings with a terse English expletive: "Nuts!"

Eddy arrives in search of his partner. He is dressed with a "loud, international bad taste which a certain North American sector has imposed on the underdeveloped nations." Supplied with a cigar and good whisky, Eddy sits down to discuss business with Gonzalo. Since both are capable of directing Diana's actions and are engaged in a mental duel for the services of the telepathist, it turns out that Diana speaks for them. In what can be termed a theatrical *tour de force*, Diana assumes the personalities of both men alternately and acts out their entire conversation while they supply the mental directions. Here López Rubio again reveals his fascination for multiple personality and employs the concept in a highly original and theatrically effective manner. The exchange continues for several minutes and Diana is indignant when she finally regains full control of her forces. She makes an important decision: to stop being a receiver and to try her hand at sending.

The action of the third act takes place the following day. Diana exercises her new powers as a sender and directs a message to Eddy to keep away from the doctor's apartment. Then she takes over the prim and proper Florita and changes her into a frivolous girl who speaks slang, smokes, and displays an unsuspected familiarity with a variety of mixed drinks. Gonzalo is amazed by the new Florita, and when she uses her pet name for him (Cuchi-Cuchi) in reference to a young man, the doctor is nonplussed. Florita becomes progressively more tipsy and finally staggers out in a state of total intoxication. Eddy arrives, and Diana uses her powers on him to persuade him to give up his contractual rights to her services in favor of Gonzalo. In a highly amusing scene, which reverses the telepathic transferal in Act II, Diana controls the words of both Gonzalo and Eddy. Each expresses himself in the manner of the young woman, employing numerous foreign expressions.

Helenio is summoned again to resume his duties as assistant to the doctor, and Diana informs him that she intends to be married the following month. Through a slight mix-up, the nurse receives the next message directed to Gonzalo and exclaims with passion: "I love you, Diana! I love you madly! . . ." When the doctor takes over and embraces Diana, the nurse delivers a brief curtain speech which shows a classical inspiration and which contains one of López Rubio's recurring thoughts on love:

To me, love seems to be one of the best modern inventions. . . . They say it's very ancient. . . . But, the truth is, if you want it to last eternally, there's no way but to reinvent it every day. . . .

Diana's Mind Is Busy lacks the serious undertones of many of López Rubio's plays, and its humor leans much more toward the farcical than toward the poetic or ironic. This does not mean that it is an inferior work. On the contrary, it is an extraordinarily fine example of humorous theater which borders on farce, and it ranks with *Not Tonight, Either* as the best-crafted and polished light comedy of the playwright's maturity. Although the funniest scenes are variations of a single device—the transferal or modification of personality through telepathic impulse—the action is not repetitious. The clever reversal of events achieved through Diana's decision to become a sender (and to show the possibility of female dominance over the male) reveals the author's practiced knowledge of theatrical effect and of female psychology as well.

II   Esta noche, tampoco
(Not Tonight, Either)

Shortly after the opening of *Not Tonight, Either* in November 1961, José Monleón, the editor of *Primer Acto* and an outspoken advocate of committed theater in Spain, expressed regret that this popular comedy was all too typical of the theater of its time.[3] He acknowledged that López Rubio was a good writer, honorably involved in his profession, but he quoted at length from the playwright's *autocrítica*, in which the author himself had described the play as "very light and very superficial."[4] (López Rubio had also added the opinion that the threat of atomic annihilation did not eliminate the need to laugh.) *Not Tonight, Either* is indeed a very light comedy; it is also extremely well conceived, hilariously satirical, and unabashedly theatrical. It was the second play that López Rubio had tailored to the talents of Conchita Montes, so it is not surprising that it abounds in opportunities for the protagonist to show intelligence, wit, and charm.

The first act of the play is set in the elegant apartment of Lucía, the Spanish wife of an American oil magnate (Williams). Arriving home at four in the morning with her ardent escort (Gustavo), Lucía finds two men asleep on her living-room sofa. In a few lines of terse exposition, it is made clear that Lucía's husband has been indifferent to her for years and that they have been leading separate lives. She recognizes one of the sleeping men as Funes, her husband's attorney and representative who signs her checks. Obviously, Gustavo must leave the apartment before the men awaken, and Lucía sends the irritated suitor back to his hotel to get some sleep.

The maid (Nati) appears and informs Lucía that Funes is bearing some bad news about Williams. Then, with Nati's assistance, Lucía stages a second entrance (minus Gustavo) to awaken Funes and his companion (Villanueva). Before the two men can reveal the purpose of their visit, the telephone rings, and Lucía engages in a short conversation with a friend which serves mainly to keep the audience in suspense. After hanging up, she astonishes the two men by telling them that they may address her as "the widow Williams." Funes and Villanueva warn Lucía that the oil company is in crisis and that the board of directors has decided to keep Williams's death a secret until a contract to exploit new oil fields is signed with the Emir of Tuwak. With some difficulty, they persuade Lucía to go along with the deception. When the attorneys leave, Lucía is left on stage alone for a moment. By looking at and touching the wedding ring on her finger she suggests to the audience that she is not unmoved by her husband's death; but her moment of seriousness is interrupted by a call from Gustavo, who wants to come back to the apartment. She refuses his request, and the act ends as she speaks the words that give the play its title: "Not tonight, either."

The second act takes place in the modern, expensive home of Lucía's friends Marisa and Felix, on the Costa del Sol. Once again Lucía enters to find Funes and Villanueva asleep on a sofa. She summons Nati, and they engage in a bit of play-acting to awaken the ubiquitous lawyers. Nati pretends to be an airline attendant giving instructions to the passengers for landing. Lucía and the two men join the "play" quite naturally, and López Rubio permits his characters to demonstrate an awareness of their own theatricalness by "performing" within the play itself.

Felix, Marisa's husband, arrives from the beach, and shortly afterwards the phone rings. It is Gustavo calling to continue his pursuit of Lucía. In an effective telephone "monologue," she assures him that their rendezvous will certainly take place now. At this point the comedy takes a decidedly Pirandellian turn, for an actor named Douglas appears in the "role" of the late Richard Williams. Lucía admits that the impersonator, who has been employed by the oil company, has achieved a striking characterization, but she suggests that he should not feel obliged to play his role when they are alone. Douglas disagrees, maintaining that it is too difficult for an actor to step in and out of character at a moment's notice. In the second scene, Douglas has become so ardent in his attentions that Lucía threatens to denounce him as an impostor; however, Funes reminds her that no one would believe her accusation and that her sanity might even be questioned. Just as Douglas is taking Lucía into his arms, Gustavo appears on the scene and rushes to her defense. But Lucía is obliged to pretend that the actor is really her husband, and her rendezvous with Gustavo must be postponed again.

The third act of *Not Tonight, Either* opens with a brief, two-page scene that seems to have been added as an afterthought—probably to satisfy the censors by demonstrating that Lucía has spent the night on the living-room sofa rather than with her substitute husband. The second scene contains an amusing exchange between Nati and Marisa's servant Pilar in which López Rubio shows his familiar skill at using flavorful popular speech for humorous effect. Then Funes and Villanueva return to tell Lucía that they have called New York and have received authorization for Douglas to terminate his impersonation and go back to Hollywood in Williams's private plane. Gustavo appears again, and Lucía agrees to meet him that night. When he leaves, Nati enters to announce the arrival of still another man who calls himself "Mister Williams." (The role is appropriately played by the same actor who portrayed Douglas-Williams in the second act.) This second false husband is accompanied by an Arab bodyguard (Abdul) who "speaks a dialect of the frontier of Kuwait with only thirty-two words." But Abdul turns out to be the Emir of Tuwak himself who, suspecting a plot by the board of directors of the oil company, has hired his own actor to impersonate his old friend Williams. His reasoning is that the impersonation would confirm the demise of Williams, since only the real Williams could top the actor's performance.

The final scene between Abdul and Lucía is the finest in the play and also one of the funniest ever written by López Rubio. Both the materialistic and the sensual aspects of the oil-rich Emir's way of life are extravagantly satirized, while Lucía is permitted to show a growing if somewhat skeptical interest in this impulsive and attractive man. Abdul proposes to her and even agrees to dispose of his other ninety-three wives and legions of concubines for the sake of his new love. He invites Lucía to his yacht; and, at the end of the play, it is clear that she intends to accept the invitation, as she tells the frustrated Gustavo over the phone that their oft-postponed rendezvous is canceled again.

Not Tonight, Either is satirical farce-comedy which in no way aspires to profundity, but all the elements in the play are skillfully measured and balanced. Theatrical interest is consistently sustained from beginning to end, and the dialogue offers some of López Rubio's cleverest repartee. At the same time, the recurring emphasis on theater-within-theater and the underlying concept of life theatricalized link this light work to the playwright's more important serious comedies of the 1950s.

III   Nunca es tarde
(It's Never Too Late)

The premiere of *It's Never Too Late* took place on October 14, 1964, in the Teatro Lara—almost three years after the opening of *Not Tonight, Either*. It was the first serious comedy (or, perhaps, "drama with comedy") that López Rubio had attempted in several years, and in the *autocrítica* he noted that the play was written "against the current trends of the theater." He also described the new work as "a play that inspires hope, between the poles of humor and poetry, with a supernatural twist [*juego*] and a perhaps annoying share of literature." [5] As usual, the playwright was accurate and to the point in stating his aims and defining his creation. Although some questions were raised about the resolution that he chose for the predicament of his protagonist in the third act, the critical reception was, on the whole, quite favorable. García Pavón praised the dramatist's skill as a writer;[6] and Marqueríe declared that the new play ranked among López Rubio's best.[7]

It's Never Too Late reveals some similarities to López Rubio's earlier serious comedies, but the obvious preoccupation with the idea of time running out and the tragic death of a principal character at the end of the second act give the work a special mood and identity. The play begins with a brief prologue set in heaven (which was omitted in the Madrid production). Two celestial voices are discussing the three aborted meetings between Flora and Miguel over a period of thirty years. Since the two are destined to meet on earth and experience a grand passion together, instructions have been for the celestial "workers" to arrange it. The first voice expresses some doubts about the success of the mission—particularly after so much time has passed—but the second voice assures him that for love "it's never too late." [8]

The first act opens in the apartment-studio of a young sculptor named Arturo. He is receiving two provincial officials who wish to commission a monument to one of their town's illustrious citizens. There is some amusing satire of taste in art, but the scene serves mainly to establish Arturo's identity and profession and to enable his aunt, Flora Vidal, to make a well-timed entrance. Flora is a retired but still-attractive opera singer to whom Arturo is almost like a son. It is quickly apparent that she is sensitive about her age, though the playwright does not present her as excessively vain or self-centered. Rather, she is a serious artist who has given everything to her career and now realizes that it is probably too late for the love that she has not experienced. Noticing that Arturo is preparing for guests, she questions him and discovers that his fiancée (María) is bringing her father (Miguel) to meet him for the first time. Since Flora considers herself Arturo's "family," she insists on remaining.

To Flora's surprise and pleasure, Miguel recognizes her as the famous star of opera and informs her that he has almost met her several times—first on an ocean liner years before, when she remained in her stateroom because of illness, and later, when he had planned to go backstage with flowers at the Metropolitan, the performance was canceled; finally, Flora had been invited to attend the wedding of Miguel to Belén, a former school friend of Flora's, and on that occasion she had sent a gift without attending. María is considerably less impressed by Arturo's colorful aunt than Miguel, and she cannot imagine that her father's interest is more than momentary fascination. However, the destined meeting of Flora and Miguel has taken place, and it proves to be the beginning of a passionate involvement.

The second act of the play takes place in the living room of a secluded house in the mountains outside Madrid where Flora and Miguel are living together. Flora enters with several "props"—a white lace mantilla, a shell comb, a bouquet of artificial flowers, and a fan—which she places on a table. When Miguel joins her, Flora pretends he is another suitor and tells him that she wants him to be many different lovers for her (an allusion to multiple personality that is not unexpected in López Rubio's plays). Then she sets the stage for a re-creation of the night that Miguel had brought her flowers and found her performance at the Metropolitan cancelled. In Flora's new "script" they will actually meet and fall in love. She puts a recording of the third act of *Carmen* on the phonograph and takes the props from the table. The bouquet of flowers is, of course, for Miguel, who must attempt to go backstage between the acts and be refused admission. After Flora plays the ending of the fourth act of the opera, Miguel presents himself backstage, and Flora momentarily assumes the "role" of the doorman who admits him. The scene is more detailed and more consciously a play-within-a-play than Beatriz's re-creation of her honeymoon with her substitute husband in *The Blindfold*, but its dramatic purpose is similar, and it clearly links this play with López Rubio's earlier serious comedies.

At the point when Miguel is about to knock at Flora's dressing-room door, their "play" is interrupted by the arrival of Arturo and María. Miguel elects to let Flora deal with the young married couple and leaves the room. María confronts Flora in a contemptuous manner, for she is incapable of accepting the idea of sensual love between two people who are so much older than she—particularly if one of them is her own father. But Flora rises to the occasion and defends the right of all people to love throughout their lives:

FLORA. (*Turning to María and smiling.*) We were talking about love. . . .
MARÍA.   What you call it, what you give that name to . . . I wouldn't call *that* love. . . .
FLORA. (*Controlling herself.*) Why not?
MARÍA.   (*Coldly.*) Because it's ridiculous.
FLORA. (*Reacting to María's words with anger.*) There is no ridiculous love! It's a lie! For those who truly love each other . . . imperfections, flaws . . . disappear.
MARÍA.   For them, perhaps. . . . But what about other people?
FLORA.   Other people! Why should they look? . . . Love is made to be seen from inside. Then there is nothing more beautiful in the world.
MARÍA.   (*Implacable.*) Even at a certain age?
FLORA. (*Excitedly.*) What age? . . . The fire is always the same. . . . What kind of life are you planning for yourself, if you limit love? . . . Don't the ugly, the crippled, the deformed, have a right to love? At your age you think love is some exclusive right.

The battle of words reaches a degree of fervor and, on María's part, harshness, unequaled in López Rubio's plays. Finally, Miguel returns to the room, and the extended verbal duel is interrupted. As he prepares to go to Madrid on business, Flora expresses her concern about his driving back. From this comment it is clear to María that her father has been staying with Flora. After Miguel's departure, Flora announces that she and Miguel have made plans to marry, and she attempts to convey the sense of urgency she has felt and her keen awareness of the passing time. The phone rings; Arturo answers and attempts to conceal the tragic news he has received. He exits briefly and then summons María to join him. Flora does not have to be told that Miguel has been killed in an automobile accident. When she is alone on stage, she begins a long and dramatic "conversation" with her dead lover in which details of the accident are conveyed to the audience. Arturo reappears without María to break the news to Flora, but she tells him she already knows, insisting that she be left "alone with him."

Between the second and third acts, there is a short *intermedio*, or interlude (like the prologue, omitted in performance), in which the celestial voices discuss Miguel's death and explain that he had swerved the car to avoid hitting a child. Ironically, the boy was already ordained to die a few days later of an incurable malady. But their mission is not over yet, for they are dealing with a love that is destined to triumph over death. The brief act is set in Flora's home in Madrid,[9] and begins with a scene between María and a physician who is treating Flora. She continues to talk with the dead Miguel and refuses to see anyone except her nephew and his wife. María remains utterly literal-minded, but the doctor attempts to explain to her how illusion can be a way to survive. Arturo is more understanding of his aunt's condition and has even begun to enjoy her "conversations" (becoming a kind of audience for her). Because of the need to make repairs in the apartment, they convince Flora that an architect must be allowed to pass through her bedroom to examine a leak in the bathroom. Reasonably enough, the doctor wonders why an architect rather than a repairman has been sent to deal with a leak—not suspecting that a supernatural plan is being implemented. Flora reluctantly agrees to let the man come in. When he appears, he bears an uncanny resemblance to Miguel.[10] Flora's reaction is immediate. She begins to open the windows that have been sealed for months; and as the sun floods the room, she looks up and, with a new interest in life, speaks her final words to Miguel: "Thank you."

The device that López Rubio uses to restore hope to Flora seems no more than a theatrical contrivance if the supernatural force behind it is not taken into consideration. When the playwright had dealt with fantasy (or the supernatural) previously, it had been so integral a part of the dramatic plan that it was easily acceptable, and suspension of disbelief was possible. The existence of Don Mateo in *Overnight* is dramatically acceptable because he is himself a principal character in the play and seems real—even though he speaks of his own nonreality; and in *The Other Shore*, the four principals become ghosts in the first moments of the comedy and are more real as spirits than the living characters who appear later; but the fantastic element of *It's Never Too Late* remains outside the frame of dramatic action and is consequently less easy to accept. The prologue informs the audience in a light manner that the meeting of Flora and Miguel is destined, but until the final moments of the second act (approximately three-quarters through the play) the supernatural has no apparent force—or at least the sequence of events requires no obvious help from above. Consequently, when Flora begins to talk with Miguel after his death, the first reaction of an audience may well be to interpret her communication with him as delusion—until specific details of the fatal accident are conveyed in Flora's monologue. The interlude between acts two and three is, of course, intended to prepare the audience for a turn of events as improbable as the arrival of Miguel's double in the person of the architect. Since both of the celestial scenes were omitted in the Madrid production, it is not surprising that García Pavón found insufficient justification for the appearance of the architect and considered the final act of the play too conventional after the dramatically intense second act.[11]

The most outstanding feature of *It's Never Too Late* is the character of Flora Vidal—one of the most credible and appealing in López Rubio's theater. She is, in a sense, a direct descendant of Gloria Velarde of *Remedy in Memory*; but whereas Gloria resorts to play-acting in desperation and confuses reality and illusion, Flora employs theater intelligently to re-create her life and to enhance her romance with Miguel. When the need arises, she is fully capable of dealing with reality. Just as Beatriz throws off her feigned madness when confronting her unfaithful husband in *The Blindfold*, Flora is unmistakably in command of her faculties when she must deal with the unthinking and brutal attacks of her lover's daughter. Though Flora is, admittedly, loquacious at times, her talk is not idle. Through this character, the playwright expresses his understanding of the loss of youth, the awareness of lost time, the conflict between the generations, and the unending and undeniable need for love. There is ample evidence of López Rubio's sense of theatrical effect and of his verbal grace throughout the play. Although not all of the elements of the work meld perfectly, *It's Never Too Late* is a comedy-drama that commands respect.

IV   La puerta del ángel *(The Way of the Angel)*

The unperformed serious drama *The Way of the Angel* is the only original work for the stage completed by López Rubio in the late 1960s. He had not attempted a play totally devoid of comedy since *Our Hands Are Innocent* in 1958; but the more recent work differs greatly in setting and dramatic approach from the earlier *comedia dramática*,[12] which had been deliberately stark in mood and rhetorical in tone. *The Way of the Angel* is highly charged and melodramatic at times, with undisguised sexual yearnings and memories of violence. And at its most dramatic moment, a level of eloquence is reached.

The play is set on the outskirts of a "sad" town in the province of León, and the playwright gives special attention to the description of the atmosphere and locale in an introductory passage of poetic effect:

It is not a room made sad only by the passing of the years or by something that has come to weigh heavily over the atmosphere. Everything was already dry and austere when it was born: the house, the lines, the colors. And the silence, and the echo of the silence. Sealed, intentionally, against the cold, and against the heat, against the sunlight, against the wind of the plain. Not against any happiness from the outside, for there is no happiness outside either. The town has the same color, and the same taste, as the land. The people have the color of the land too, if they work it, or the waxy pallor of recluses. For their attire no color other than black is conceivable. There is not even the memory of laughter. The children do not learn to laugh. Crimes are admitted, but not sins. God is only a constant but distant fear.[13]

The entire action of the play takes place in the sitting room of Martirio, a woman of fifty who dresses as if she were in mourning. She is accompanied by Norberta, a somewhat younger servant who obviously enjoys a special power over her mistress. The third member of the household is an attractive young servant girl named Aúrea. Blond and blue-eyed, she stands in contrast to the somber older women. Early in the play, Norberta demands money from Martirio, but the nature of her blackmail—which has been going on for some fifteen years—is not revealed.

The two women begin a pathetic ritual that recalls some of the inventions and fantasies of López Rubio's serious comedies, although in the charades of Norberta and Martirio there is not the slightest suggestion of humor. Every Friday they receive imaginary callers, for people have long since stopped coming to the house. Norberta announces the arrival of Don Félix, the mayor, and Martirio pours coffee for the nonexistent guest as she addresses an empty chair. She creates the "script" as she goes along, and she discovers that the mayor's wife has not accompanied him this particular night because the weather is bad. The women pretend to hear the doorbell, and the second imaginary visitor, Doña Andrea, arrives. As the scene progresses, López Rubio subtly reveals something of Martirio's past history: she is a widow and has maintained that she will never marry again because she had had so perfect a husband—or such is the false legend she has created.

For the third time, the two women pretend to hear the doorbell, and Martirio suggests that it must be the priest. There is a momentary suspension of Martirio's "play" as some of her deeper frustrations break through the pretense. Suddenly the doorbell actually rings, creating a terrible anxiety in both women as well as suspense for the audience. Norberta ushers in Julián, a man of forty whose appearance betrays his physical and mental exhaustion. He has been released from prison for good conduct after serving fifteen years of a sentence for the murder of Martirio's husband.

The doorbell rings again. Julián hides, and the real Don Félix enters to warn Martirio that Julián has been released. He urges her to move into a house she owns within the town for her own safety, but she refuses. After Don Félix's departure, Julián shows a commanding attitude toward the women. When he is alone with Martirio and takes her face between his hands, it is apparent that they had once been lovers. She attempts to persuade him to leave and to live in another city, where she can visit him regularly. Martirio exits to get money for her lover, and Norberta returns. She tells Julián that she has overheard the conversation and declares her own passion for him. Don Félix appears again and informs the women that he has posted guards around the house for their protection—a significant piece of information that will affect the outcome of the play. Now it is impossible for Julián to leave. Martirio begins to laugh hysterically, and Aúrea, awakened by the commotion, appears in the doorway. Julián is immediately drawn to her, and the act ends as he asks: "Who is she?"

In the second act, there is a struggle between Martirio and Norberta for Julián's attentions, and their sexual yearnings for him are suggested both in their manner and their frenzied counterplotting. But it is the gentle Aúrea who begins to instill new hope in Julián. In a long and moving speech addressed to her he tells of his utter disillusionment, the years of loneliness in prison, and how he had learned to read. In books he had made discoveries that had been denied him in the years in which he had been illiterate:

JULIÁN.   . . . Fifteen years. Can you understand that? Can anyone? How many days there are and how many nights? And how many times you clench your teeth to keep from crying out? . . . You can be the way of my salvation. I read in a book . . . I learned to read inside there, and I read all that I could. There are a lot of books. Do you know how many? (*Aúrea shakes her head.*) More than anyone can count. I once asked a man who looked after the library. And he told me thousands and thousands. Like trees. Can you imagine? . . . I read that a man has only two ways, at certain moments, when life seizes him and presses down on him like a closing fist. The way of the Angel and the way of the Devil. Until now I've known nothing but hell. For God's sake, understand. . . . You can be my way of the Angel.[14]

It is finally disclosed that Julián had been the lover of both Norberta and Martirio when he first arrived at the house as a hired hand of twenty. Martirio herself had committed the murder when her elderly husband had discovered her relationship with the young man. Now Julián is determined to leave with Aúrea to begin a new life. He decides to take money from Martirio—a small compensation for his years of incarceration for a crime he did not commit. Martirio thinks that Norberta has robbed her and confronts her; Norberta calls out for help, and a shot is heard. Aúrea has run out the door in fear and has been killed by the guards outside. Julián accuses Norberta of intentionally causing the girl's death, but he is doomed to remain in the house with the two possessive women for whom he can feel only disgust.

The present ending of the play is not totally convincing, and Julián's acceptance of "captivity" is less than credible after the changes he has undergone. Dissatisfied with this ending, López Rubio has considered a new and more forceful resolution in which Julián escapes from the house, having found his "way of the Angel"— even though he has tragically lost the innocent woman who has been his salvation. Then Martirio and Norberta return to the identical hermetic existence they were living in the opening scene of the play and to their invented reality in which they receive imaginary callers on Fridays.[15]

The Way of the Angel is perhaps the most "Spanish" of López Rubio's plays, with its provincial background. Dogmatic custom and unbending attitudes are determining forces in the actions of the principals much as in Lorca's *The House of Bernarda Alba*; but the play is not poetic in the same sense as Lorca's famous work—though it does qualify as a drama of poeticized reality. The emphasis on sexuality and the use of sexual desire as a prime motivating force make this drama unique among López Rubio's works for the stage. Indeed, the frank treatment of sexual motivation and the resultant violence undoubtedly prevented the play's production at the time of its composition. Although events of the second act are perhaps too complex and the tone too melodramatic, with the revised ending contemplated by the playwright, *The Way of the Angel* may eventually receive the staging it merits.

V   El corazón en la mano
(With Heart in Hand)

In October 1971, López Rubio returned to the theater with an adaptation of his short television play *Veneno activo* (Active Poison);[16] a few months later, on March 23, 1972, a new full-length original work of his had its premiere. Although *With Heart in Hand* did not enjoy a long run, it commanded critical respect, and López Rubio was awarded both the National Prize for Drama for the 1971–72 season and the yearly drama award of the newspaper *El Alcázar*. In his review for *A B C*, Adolfo Prego called the new work "a captivating play . . . which is among the three best that López Rubio has written." [17] While Prego's hierarchy of plays might be debated, *With Heart in Hand* is a well-conceived and timely drama in which the playwright demonstrates his ability to write effectively in the idiom of the 1970s.

Divided into two acts and five scenes of varying length, *With Heart in Hand* represents a departure from the more conventional three-act form that López Rubio had favored so frequently in the past. The first act is set in the modest and rather depressing office of Eduardo, a middle-aged businessman of ordinary appearance whom the playwright describes as "a good man for the moment." [18] He is joined by his secretary, Leopoldina, a loyal but frustrated woman who resents the subservient role she has had to accept in the business world because of her sex. The company that Eduardo has inherited from his father is on the verge of bankruptcy, but he has steadfastly rejected certain deals that would require a compromise of his moral standards. Leopoldina reveals a far more realistic understanding of the situation than her employer, and she warns him that he cannot do business with his heart. The brief opening scene ends with the introduction of a new character (Mapy) by telephone—a recourse not unexpected in López Rubio's theater. But the only precise information disclosed is that Mapy is a girl who has broken an appointment with Eduardo to be with her friends.

The second scene takes place a few days later. A conniving inter-mediary named Troncoso attempts to persuade Eduardo to use his influence with a prominent cousin to promote a deal in which he has an interest. The indignant Eduardo throws him out of the office and tears up the business card he has left. Leopoldina carefully retrieves the pieces from the wastebasket as she urges Eduardo to reconsider. Mapy, who proves to be a pretty but not particularly intelligent girl of twenty, arrives carrying a guitar. She enters the office against Leopoldina's wishes, and there is a humorous exchange between the two women of different ages and different experiences in life.

Eduardo is in love with Mapy and is irritated by her use of "don" with his first name and the formal "usted" (you) with which she addresses him. In an especially well-written scene, the older man confesses his love to the carefree young woman. Attempting to show her the depth of his feelings, he reaches inside his shirt and symbolic-ally removes his heart and hands it to her. Such a poetic gesture is incomprehensible to Mapy, and she informs Eduardo that the real purpose of her visit is to persuade him to give her boyfriend (Rogelio) a job in the office. When Eduardo agrees, she gives him a kiss of appreciation, but rejects his attempt to embrace her.[19] This painful rejection by Mapy marks the beginning of Eduardo's determination to change his life, and the first step is to contact Troncoso.

In the final scene of the first act, Eduardo receives Troncoso and begins to cash in on his years of integrity by lending his aid to the questionable deal. Rogelio, a perfect representative of his generation in his casual dress and mastery of the language of the moment, arrives for an interview. He is not eager to become a part of the *"sociedad de consumo"* (consumer society), and he also fears that he will be ex-pected to marry Mapy as a condition of his employment. But Eduardo assures him that this is not the case. On the contrary, he must discourage Mapy's interest in matrimony.

At the beginning of the second act, there is a striking change both in Eduardo's appearance and in his surroundings. He is now attired in expensive, tailor-made clothes, and his movements suggest a confi-dence that was lacking in his days of failure. The office has been moved to a modern building and its décor bespeaks success. Rogelio has also undergone a noticeable change; his hair is shorter, his attire more conservative, and he has acquired certain materialistic in-terests. Only Leopoldina seems relatively unaltered by the obvious change of fortune. For her, the transformation of her honest but unsuccessful employer has been far more drastic than she had anticipated. She is wary of Mapy's influence and warns Eduardo that the girl is "empty inside" and unworthy of his love. When Eduardo turns sarcastic in his replies, she accuses him of not having a heart (which is figuratively true). Leopoldina is actually jealous of the younger woman, and she admits that she had believed that Eduardo would eventually marry her. He, in turn, declares that his feelings had never gone beyond compassion for the plain but loyal secretary. At this point Leopoldina might well have become an object of pity, but the playwright avoids pathos by adding a touch of humor which reveals her inner strength and ability to endure.

Even Troncoso is troubled by Eduardo's enthusiasm for acquiring money with little concern for the ethics of a transaction; and Rogelio expresses surprise that the man Mapy had described as an "angel" is capable of business arrangements that might be termed "irregular." Mapy continues to reject Eduardo's attentions and blames him for Rogelio's indifference toward her. The capricious girl is now beginning to fantasize about marriage and security. She expresses feelings that suggest she may actually be in love with Rogelio—though she is unable to define her own emotions.

In the fifth and final scene of *With Heart in Hand*, Rogelio announces to Eduardo that he intends to leave Madrid. Mapy has told him that she is pregnant, and he has no desire to be trapped in marriage. After Rogelio's departure, a troubled man named Hernández arrives to consult with Eduardo. He has borrowed money at high interest and is unable to repay the loan. Eduardo shows no compassion for him as he pleads for more time. When Hernández admits that he is contemplating suicide, Eduardo responds with cruel sarcasm and sends the pitiable man away. Then Mapy enters to tell Eduardo that she is not really certain about her pregnancy (or the possible father), and Eduardo offers to marry her. Her reaction is more like that of a pleased child than a woman faced with a serious problem. She remembers that she has brought something for him which she had found "while rummaging through a closet." It is his heart, which she is returning in a gift box. Eduardo opens his shirt and puts his heart back in its normal place, and a moment later Leopoldina appears to inform him that Hernández has returned. This time Eduardo reacts quite differently to the man's predicament. He gives him the time he needs to repay the loan and even tears up their agreement.

Eduardo has persuaded Mapy to go off with him for a weekend, and Leopoldina—momentarily representing Eduardo's con-

science—invents an excuse for him to cancel the trip. Still obsessed
by the girl, he rejects his secretary's advice and proposed remedy. As
Mapy waits for him outside the office, he goes through the motions of
removing his heart again and crushes it in his hand. Having made an
irrevocable decision, he opens the window and symbolically tosses
out the damaged heart.

With Heart in Hand lacks the element of hope that is invariably
present in the resolutions of López Rubio's most memorable serious
comedies, and the central character displays a degree of self-interest
that is unexpected. There is a suggestion of a modern Faust in the
character of Eduardo, as he sells his good name for the material
success that he believes will enable him to win the love of a girl who is
probably incapable of loving. Symbolically, he hands his heart (if not
his soul) over to her—an act that allows him to engage in business
without the interference of his feelings and to respond in the most
callous way to a victim such as Hernández. When Mapy returns his
heart and he replaces it, he is once again capable of showing compassion. But, ultimately, Eduardo is swayed by his desire to possess
Mapy, and through his final symbolic gesture destroys all possibility
of being ruled by his emotions in the future. (His rejection of genuine
love is, in a sense, a denial of the message contained in *It's Never Too
Late*.) The irony of Eduardo's decision is, of course, that it is made on
behalf of the uncomprehending and insensitive Mapy.

With Heart in Hand provides further evidence of López Rubio's
ability to deal with themes and dramatic situations that differ considerably from those of the masterfully wrought serious comedies and
lighter satirical works that brought him success. While polished and
graceful dialogue, touches of irony, and poetic undercurrents are
notable features in this play, structurally and thematically it is the
most atypical produced work that the playwright had written since
Our Hands Are Innocent.

CHAPTER 8

Theater for Television

I   Al filo lo imposible
(At the Edge of the Impossible)

WHATEVER its artistic and literary worth, a television play rarely commands the kind of critical attention routinely given to a work for the stage. Although television productions are now generally preserved on videotape, opportunities for repeated viewings of most serious dramatic shows are limited to an occasional rerun at best. Fortunately, the scripts of the sixteen episodes of López Rubio's first original series for television, *At the Edge of the Impossible*, have been published, and it is possible to evaluate them individually and collectively.[1] First shown in 1969, the series was awarded the most prestigious prizes designated for the medium in Spain—the Premio Ondas and the National Award for Television Drama.

While the title of the series may suggest a continuing group of related episodes, López Rubio's plays are actually short, individual "teleplays" which, with the exception of one two-part comedy, are self-contained, with no characters or situations that are repeated. What most of them do have in common is an unusual plot, denouement, or dramatically arresting twist that places the action close to "the edge of the impossible." In this respect they are comparable in spirit to some (not all) of the stories and sketches of López Rubio's first published book, *Unlikely Tales*. However, all of the plays lie within the realm of possibility and none could be considered pure fantasy.[2]

In spite of the variety of themes and situations represented in the episodes, the level of dramatic interest is notably sustained throughout the series. Indeed, *At the Edge of the Impossible* offers examples of writing that are, on a smaller scale, comparable to the best work that the playwright has created for the stage. In some instances, theatrical recourses that can be found in his major serious comedies have been effectively adapted for the special and different demands of television drama in which visual suggestion is paramount. Like the

119

stage works, each of the television plays—which range from ingenious comedy to poetically realistic drama—should be considered in
terms of the author's artistic and dramatic intent.

Two of the humorous teleplays—the dual-episode *El secuestro*
(The Kidnapping) /*El rescate* (The Ransoming) and *Moneda falsa*
(Counterfeit Counterfeit), deal with hilariously inept ventures into
crime, with dialogue and situations that are reminiscent of longer
stage works of Jardiel Poncela and Mihura. Although relatively brief
of necessity, they are in no way inferior to the theatrical works of this
genre by López Rubio's two late contemporaries. *The Kidnapping/
The Ransoming* is the more complex and more interesting of the two
plays because of its length, which permits a more extended development of the dramatic situation. The principal character is a young
man named Aurelio who is abducted by four bungling kidnappers
who mistake him for a millionaire from Florida (Pachín Rodríguez).
Inadvertently, Aurelio finds himself involved in the second (and
successful) attempt to kidnap Rodríguez. He gains influence with the
kidnappers and begins to enjoy playing at nonconformity and crime.
The group is frustrated again when Rodríguez's wife refuses to
believe that the abduction is more than a ruse by her husband.

In a scene that recalls the enthusiasm of The Buyer in López
Rubio's *The Blindfold* for the unconventional household he has entered, Aurelio talks with his wife by phone and invents an excuse to
remain away from home—crime being far more exciting than middle-
class routine. The abducted Rodríguez also enjoys the company of his
captors and requests that they keep him until after his birthday
celebration. The eventual undoing of the amateur criminals is tied to
the "tragic flaw" of one of them: robbing pay phones. Finally, both
Rodríguez and Aurelio return to "reality," but the latter's life is made
more promising by the millionaire's offer of a job in Florida. As in
Mihura's *Tres sombreros de copa* (Three Top Hats), the lure of the
unconventional is contrasted with the dulling routine of ordinary life;
but in the case of Aurelio, the flirtation with crime at least provides
the chance for a change in his future life.

Counterfeit Counterfeit is comparable to the two-part crime play
in the quality of its dialogue and humor, though its basic plot is
simpler and less engrossing, and the element of psychological involvement is lacking. The shorter work is concerned with the supremely naive attempts of a picturesque family group to become
counterfeiters. They fail abysmally, first because the cost of producing each bill is greater than the value of the denomination decided
upon (100 pesetas). They move on to 500-peseta notes, requiring a

different size of paper and added cost. Their final—and absurdly improbable—solution is to invent a new denomination of a 1,125-peseta note to assure themselves a "margin of profit." No one is deceived, and three of the bunglers are apprehended immediately.

New qualities that are in evidence in the several of the teleplays are dark, or sardonic, humor and dramatic situations that are only a step away from the macabre. *La casi viuda* (Almost a Widow) deals affectingly with the strange arrangement between a man who has had a heart transplant and the widow of the donor to enable her to "talk" with her deceased husband. *Antes y después* (Before and After) offers one of the more unusual dramatic situations attempted by the playwright. López Rubio describes the two characters (Jerónimo and Damián) of the short drama as "two vagabonds, similar to those in Mingote's drawings." [3] Damián murders an old man who catches him in the act of robbing his home. The next morning, Jerónimo appears while Damián is preparing coffee over an open fire. He claims to be able to see the past, and Damián counters that he can foresee the future. Jerónimo proves his abilities by telling of an ancient battle that had been fought on the spot and by finding a rusty sword from another era; Damián predicts that oil wells will one day cover the same field. When Jerónimo describes Damián's crime of the night before and demands half the money, the murderer refuses. As Jerónimo walks down the railroad tracks to report the crime to the Civil Guard, Damián foresees his antagonist's death under the wheels of the 10:20 train.

Also in a darker vein is *Quinientos mil ejemplares* (Five Hundred Thousand Copies), which traces the misfortunes of an unsuccessful writer from the provinces. His poems, essays, and play are rejected by a former friend who is now a prominent publisher. When his novel is rejected too, he is subjected to a barrage of pseudointellectual criticism and urged to add something violent to his experience to enable him to write a book that is salable. Driven beyond endurance, he turns on the publisher and his two readers and shoots all three. He goes to the gallows famous, leaving behind a very wealthy widow. López Rubio's satire of mass taste and those who pander to such taste while attempting to influence the creative process is scathing.

Two of the teleplays touch on religion or a religious experience. *La parroca* (The Priest's Wife)—playfully described as an "Iberian fantasy" which "occurs in Spain within a few years and most certainly never"—deals humorously with the negative effects of a priest's wife on his ministry. Eventually, the priest writes to his bishop in desperation, urging him to consider the implementation of divorce. [4] *Renglón*

122 JOSÉ LÓPEZ RUBIO

torcido (In Roundabout Ways), a more subtle work, offers a highly original plot in which a bullying service-station attendant (Antonio), who boasts of his macho qualities, is transformed into a religious lay brother by a prank of an ingenious coworker (Blas). The latter attaches a microphone to a radio in Antonio's room and speaks as the voice of God when Antonio returns home after a night of carousing. Later, he wants to tell Antonio the truth, but the changed man does not give him the opportunity. Antonio insists that God works in roundabout ways, and Blas is left in wonderment. He, too, has been changed "in a roundabout way." Although Antonio's conversion might seem improbable, it is both plausible and intriguing in López Rubio's skillful treatment, which begins mischievously and ends on a serious note.

One of the plays, *Veneno activo* (Active Poison)—a black comedy on the theme of murder, in which the dialogue is deliberately and humorously distorted to sound like a bad translation into Spanish from French—was adapted for the stage and opened at the Café-teatro Stefanis on October 21, 1971. Somewhat more static than the other episodes of the series, and with fewer pure visual effects, *Active Poison* required only minor changes for effective stage production. The intimate nature of the action (there are only two principal characters) proved well suited to the tiny stage of the café-theater.[5] As no new work by López Rubio had been produced in Madrid in almost seven years, *Active Poison* was awaited with particular interest; and, in its new form, it received more detailed critical attention than it had commanded as an episode in a television series. Critics applauded the playwright's return, and audiences enjoyed the special humor of this minor but imaginative piece of theater. Josefina Carabias wrote the most perceptive review of the opening, describing certain details of the presentation and revealing a good understanding of author's intent:

The action takes place in France. This is logical since it is a satire of "vaudeville"—that is, a caricature of what is already a caricature in itself. Therefore, the author begins to create farce even before the play begins—I was about to say before the curtain rises, forgetting that there's no curtain in café-theaters—when he announces over a loudspeaker that "we should not be surprised to hear a lot of Gallicisms and all kinds of strange locutions, since the play is poorly translated." [6]

Perhaps the most striking plays from the series (both dealing in individual ways with loneliness and old age) are *El último hilo* (The Last Connection) and *Su gran amor* (Their Great Love).[7] In these two teleplays, the dramatist utilizes techniques and develops themes that are associated particularly with some of his major serious comedies—though neither of the shorter works fits into the seriocomic category. López Rubio's use of the telephone for major dramatic functions in his plays began with *The Blindfold*; in *The Last Connection*, the instrument acquires a more important role in the action than in any previous work.[8] Doña Rosa, the central character, is an elderly widow who alleviates her terrible loneliness by answering newspaper advertisements by telephone with considerable grace and style. Although her personal finances have dwindled, she pretends to be wealthy and interested in buying expensive objects or renting a villa for the summer. When she picks up the phone one evening to make another of the calls that have become essential to her illusion and, consequently, to her survival, there is no dial tone. The telephone company has cut off her service, and she is struck with despair, for her funds are exhausted. As the play ends, Doña Rosa sits alone, slowly twisting the phone cord around her neck.

Their Great Love deals with the transformation of illusion into a new level of reality and the triumph (at least momentarily) of illusion—again recalling certain aspects of *The Blindfold*. Specifically, the play traces the creation of a legend around a famous theatrical personality and the eventual acceptance of the legend as truth. The opening scene provides a clever use of television-within-television, with a shot of a small TV screen on which a newscaster is announcing the death of the renowned Blanca Nevares, an opera star of the past, in a plane crash. An elegant, elderly man (Adolfo) tells a barman that he had known Blanca, and the barman in turn tells a reporter, who seeks an interview with Adolfo. The old man insists that stories of Blanca's love life have been slanderous and maintains that she really gave all for her art. After debunking the existing legends, he confides that he himself was the real and secret love of the singer's life. From a newspaper story the new legend grows, leading to a television interview (another type of television-within-television) and, ultimately, to a film based on Blanca's life. Adolfo is hired to assure the authenticity of the production and is present on the set during the filming. At one point, he interrupts a shot to instruct a young actor how to kiss the actress who is performing the role of Blanca.

The night of the premiere, Blanca reappears incognito. She had not been on the plane that had crashed because she had become interested in the driver of the cab in which she was riding to the airport. She goes to Adolfo's house, and he explains to her why he had become involved in a deception that had gotten out of hand:

ADOLFO. I don't know how to tell you. . . . I was very lonely. I was
beginning to feel as if I no longer had a right to keep on living, in a world in
which I'd become a kind of intruder. . . . Not a single reason for living.
. . . No love. . . . No children. . . . No occupation. . . . And, almost no
money. . . .

In this final scene—one of the most affecting in López Rubio's
theater—Adolfo tells Blanca that he would have settled for being only
one of many in her life, admits his great attraction to her, and
apologizes for being unable to control the legend he had begun.
Blanca is not unaffected by his words, and she chooses to join his
"play" of her life, in which their eyes had met fifty years earlier in the
Retiro Park. As Adolfo impetuously begins to retrace his (now her)
version of the story, Blanca reaches out, draws him to her, and kisses
him. In this remarkable short play, López Rubio has integrated a
favorite device, the play-within-a-play, in several guises, ultimately
employing it, as in *The Blindfold,*to create a new kind of reality. In
the stage play, the illusion provided the means for achieving a new
and more authentic existence for the protagonist; in *Their Great
Love*, it creates the final "truth" that defeats time.

With full understanding of the power of visual and aural suggestion
in the medium of television, López Rubio has supplied detailed
instructions for camera shots, special effects, montages, complemen-
tary sound effects, and off-camera voices for the episodes of *At the
Edge of the Impossible.*While all of the works contain superb dialogue, it is the masterful combination of words and the visual that
gives these plays their distinction.[9]

II   Mujeres insólitas *(Exceptional Women)*

López Rubio's second television series, *Exceptional Women*, was a
more ambitious undertaking than *At the Edge of the Impossible.* Not
only were the episodes themselves longer (one hour in performance
time) but they also represented an entirely new approach to theater
for the dramatist. The idea for a series of dramas centered on the lives
of unusual women began when Chicho Ibáñez Serrador, the director
of programming for Spanish National Television, contacted the playwright to discuss the possibility of a new continuing program.[10]
López Rubio decided to attempt a group of historical plays dealing
with women whose roles in history had been very individualistic or
whose lives had become legends—usually with the help of novelists

and playwrights of the past; and an essential part of his dramatic purpose would be a demythification based on careful historical research. It was a welcome opportunity for the playwright to combine for an artistic purpose his longtime hobby of history,[11] his wide knowledge of literature, and his special talent for creating theatrically arresting (and demanding) roles for actresses.

In an extensive interview describing the genesis, writing, and production of *Exceptional Women*, López Rubio emphasized that stage, film, and television require very distinct approaches:

Television is a new element to which the writer must adapt, since it requires a technique and structure different from those of the theater. The writer adapted to films, and to radio, and now he must adapt to television. Theater is at the heart of it all, but a theater with other dimensions. One can't do theater [for the stage] in films, nor films in television. It is very important that the writer know the medium for which his work is intended.[12]

López Rubio had clearly demonstrated, of course, in *At the Edge of the Impossible* that he understood the requirements of effective theater for television, but he had employed techniques that were familiar. *Exceptional Women*, however, is deliberately and startlingly antirealistic, with the central character of each episode stepping in and out of the action and commenting on the interpretations others have made of her story and of the words attributed to her. One of the most distinctive features of the dramas is the presence of the stage manager, Pepe, who not only supplies properties and costumes for the performers in each play but also assumes various roles as the exceptional women recall (and correct) the most dramatic events of their lives.[13] López Rubio describes him as "a combination of the stage men of the Chinese theater and the 'attrezzistas' (stage costumers) of the Spanish Golden Age." [14]

The subjects of the fourteen episodes of *Exceptional Women* include the internationally famous (Alphonsine Plessis or Camille, Cleopatra, and Lola Montes), women who have been prominent in Iberian history and literature (Inés de Castro, Juana la Loca, and the Princess of Eboli), and relatively obscure but fascinating figures (Marguerite Steinheil, Teresa Cabarrús, and the Marquise de Brinvilliers).[15] All of the plays have identical beginnings. Pepe, the stage manager, enters with a few articles of clothing and props that suggest the character and the historical epoch of the action. The exceptional woman—always referred to in the script as "Ella" (She)—enters attired in a simple evening dress. She addresses Pepe and begins to make up for her performance. She then turns to the camera and begins to tell her story in the first person directly to the audience. As the playwright has pointed out, all these characters are now "beyond good and evil" and can talk of their lives with dispassion—and even amusement at the distortions of truth.[16]

As "She" touches on significant or particularly dramatic events, these are enacted with the help of Pepe, who introduces other characters as they appear and, on occasion, participates in the action himself. "She" walks in and out of the scenes at will. Characters who do not speak, such as the members of the court in the scene that depicts the placing of the dead Inés de Castro on the throne of Portugal, are frequently mannequins dressed in the manner of the period, with costumes made of paper or cellophane. Cleopatra's barge is shown as a model or drawing, as the actress portraying the Egyptian queen reads the words that the Roman poet Lucan wrote to describe her. (Cleopatra finds Lucan somewhat overstated.) It was López Rubio's intent that literal representation be avoided to challenge the viewer and to destroy the conventional relationship of the viewer to the television screen.

Most of the exceptional women have been the subject of literature, and their lives have been romanticized and events altered or even invented by novelists, poets, and playwrights to suit their literary or dramatic purposes. And, of course, certain actions have been viewed differently in different centuries. These treatments of their stories are analyzed or commented on by the women themselves and their degree of veracity (or, more often, lack of veracity) exposed. Portions of scenes from well-known dramas are interwoven at times into the teleplays. Cleopatra acknowledges the merits of Shakespeare's depiction of her relationship with Antony, and she instructs the actor who portrays her lover to join her in the opening scene of *Antony and Cleopatra*. In *La reina loca* (The Mad Queen), a scene from Tamayo y Baus's romantic drama *Locura de amor* (Madness from Love) is performed in the style and décor of the nineteenth century. Later, Juana's lines from the death scene of the same play are spoken, but "She" comments that her speech was in reality much more natural. The episode also contains a scene with Cardinal Cisneros from Montherlant's *Le Cardinal d'Espagne* (The Cardinal of Spain) and a paraphrase of a section of Galdos's *Santa Juana de Castilla* (Saint Joan of Castile).

López Rubio's characterizations of the fourteen women are credible, whatever their national origins. His Inés de Castro is a believable woman in love, and her "testimony" to the audience (or viewer) is particularly effective; his Cleopatra is certainly as plausible as any other depiction of the famed seductress, from Shakespeare to Alfonso Paso.[17] Alphonsine Plessis ("La Dame aux Camélias" or "Camille") is more affecting in López Rubio's treatment than in Alexandre Dumas's lachrymose play or Verdi's opera, as she corrects the legend:

HER VOICE.   There was no love scene, nor operatic duet. . . . My death was for me alone, silent, almost modest. . . . I had just passed my twenty-third birthday. A good age for the beginning of a legend.[18]

Alphonsine adds further that the auction of her personal belongings produced enough money to pay her debts and that there was even some left over for a niece in Normandy (on condition that the girl never set foot in Paris). The final words of the play are given to Dumas himself, the actual lover of the "real" Camille:

VOICE OF ALEXANDRE.   . . . She was one of the few women of her type who had feelings. Doubtless, that's why she died young. She did not live the adventure that I would later attribute to Marguerite Gautier. If Marguerite didn't sacrifice anything to Armand, it was because Armand didn't love her. She would have given everything for one love, the true love, of her life. She was never called "The Lady of the Camelias." I gave that name to her; it was pure fantasy. Still, if you ask for the tomb of "The Lady of the Camelias" in the Montmartre cemetery in Paris, the guard will take you to a stone on which there is only a name. . . .
(*The camera turns and descends to a close-up of the grave. On the stone is the name "Alphonsine Plessis" and a white camelia.*) On the marble there has never been missing since then a white camelia. The divine aspect of Art is what it creates—or what it brings back to life.[19]

The playwright does not hesitate to give his own interpretation of his characters, but he does not depart from historical fact in the specific aspects of their lives. And, expectedly, he may add a note of humor or irony to a story that is generally considered to be "tragic." López Rubio acknowledges his familiarity with the distinctly personal views of history in plays by Shaw (*Caesar and Cleopatra, Androcles and the Lion*), Sherwood (*The Road to Rome*), and Anouilh (*The Lark, Beckett*),[20] but he is in no way imitative of these dramatists. The plays of *Exceptional Women* bear a very individualistic stamp both in form and in style of language. They are also a logical continuation of López Rubio's concern for illusion and reality, since in the treatments of the lives of his characters he uses as a backdrop the illusion of fiction so that the biographical facts stand out in relief as reality.

In the actual taping of the episodes, under the direction of Cayetano Luca de Tena, there were some departures from the playwright's original ideas—though none so important as to alter the basic
dramatic intent. López Rubio had thought of the possibility of a single
actress performing all of the unusual protagonists in the series. As it
turned out, a different actress was cast in each episode; but these
included some of Spain's most accomplished contemporary performers. Teresa Rabal was featured in the first episode, *La segunda señora
Tudor* (The Second Mrs. Tudor, Anne Boleyn); Julia Gutiérrez Caba
essayed the role of Juana la Loca; Carmen de la Maza was Inés de
Castro; and María Massip was Teresa Cabarrús.

There is no question but that writing *Exceptional Women* renewed
the playwright's enthusiasm for creative work at a fortunate moment.
Censorship was in retreat when he began the plays, enabling him to
write with greater freedom; and as less conventional dramatic forms
were becoming acceptable in the Spanish theater, he concluded that
viewers would respond favorably to his experiments in antirealistic
television drama. Although the original series was limited to fourteen
episodes, López Rubio has continued his research and has completed
documentation for some fifty other "exceptional women," including
Sarah Bernhardt, Calamity Jane, Mata Hari, the biblical Judith,
Isolde, and Marilyn Monroe.

López Rubio's biographical plays for Spanish television represent
an important addition to his body of dramatic writing. It would be
possible to single out numerous other examples of excellent television drama dealing with historical personages or events from both
Europe and the United States, as well as notable continuing series of
related episodes. However, no major series to date compares with
López Rubio's fourteen carefully researched dramas for *Exceptional
Women* in terms of historical scope and originality, nor have other
writers for the medium risked so complete a departure from visual
realism and conventional dramatic verisimilitude.

CHAPTER 9

Conclusion: An Overview

JOSÉ López Rubio has enjoyed one of the most varied careers of any writer of his time. Although he is principally known as a playwright, his talents as a short-story writer and novelist were ably demonstrated in works published before he was twenty-five years old. For five years, he was a film scenarist in the United States and later directed and wrote for films in Spain. Since the beginning of his second career in the theater in 1949, eighteen of his plays have had premieres in Madrid and Barcelona, and several have been produced outside Spain. His translations and adaptations of foreign plays are numerous and range from Molière to contemporary American musicals. In 1969 he began to devote himself to serious television drama, and with his two series of teleplays to date he has added a new dimension to his creative art.

Because of his long identification with the theater, López Rubio's early prose works have been overlooked in considerations of his career, but in both *Unlikely Tales* and *Roque Six* certain themes developed in his later plays are already apparent: the concept of multiple personality; feigned or real insanity; and illusion, or fantasy, that becomes reality. After his first successful collaboration with Eduardo Ugarte, López Rubio appeared as a new and promising talent, with insight into human personality and a skill for polished dialogue. His second play with Ugarte (*The House of Cards*) revealed a capacity for treating a more realistic situation effectively and a desire to introduce more modern concepts of staging to the Spanish theater. Some of the themes and ideas that López Rubio would deal with in the plays of his second career are also evident in these early collaborative efforts: the psychology of male-female relationships, the role of illusion in human behavior, the effects of illusion on personality, and the nature of personality itself. Already the dramatist saw life as being theatricalized, as something to be acted by each individual on his personal stage, and the concept becomes a major focal point in his later works, resulting in varied and original uses of the play-within-a-play.

129

At the beginning of his second career in 1949, López Rubio began to cultivate a type of serious comedy with poetic undercurrents that enhanced the literary quality of these plays. *Alberto, In August We Play the Pyrenees, The Blindfold,* and *The Other Shore* are all works of this type. Neither pure comedy nor approaching tragedy, they are, nevertheless, works of serious intent which provoke thought about the human condition, and Abel's term "metaplay" may be appropriately applied to them.[1] At the same time, the playwright experimented with plays that were less humoristic—most effectively with *Remedy in Memory,* and less successfully with *Christmas Dinner.* In 1958, López Rubio wrote his first drama of tragic implications, the totally atypical *Our Hands Are Innocent;* but in spite of wide critical interest in the work, he made a complete about-face, and his next two plays were a pair of light farcical comedies.

From that point, he began to write less frequently for the stage, and each work had its own special qualities. *It's Never Too Late* resembled the earlier serious comedies in some respects but it also had darker concerns that set it apart from the comic-poetic plays; the unproduced *The Way of the Angel* was a rural drama of violence and frank sexual motivations; and his most recent play, *With Heart in Hand,* dealt with the transformation of a man of integrity who compromises his ideals for material gain and to possess a girl who is incapable of loving him. The television plays are a major addition to López Rubio's body of work. *At the Edge of the Impossible* offers a variety of outstanding dramatic treatments; *Exceptional Women,* with its liberal use of techniques of alienation and distancing and remarkable historical scope, represents perhaps the most important step in the playwright's career since his return to the theater in 1949.

López Rubio's talent for writing graceful, witty, and ironic dialogue has been noted by critics throughout his career, and at times the dialogue has redeemed his lesser works. The fluent lines of his plays, sometimes flavored with epigrammatic passages, have caused him to be compared with Oscar Wilde. However, despite this obvious virtue in López Rubio's plays, silent visual actions and suggestions are frequently quite as relevant to his dramatic intent as the spoken word and are further evidence of an exceptional sense of the theatrical. Such actions are carefully detailed in the stage directions, and descriptions of characters, reactions and interactions of characters, details of stage setting, and descriptions of objects that complement the dramatic action are explicit and must be taken into consideration in any evaluation of his plays. In his television dramas, his instructions for camera shots (close-up, long shot, montage, fades, etc.), and the detailed instructions for the unconventional costuming and properties for the episodes of *Exceptional Women* are again a part of his aesthetic aim and are inseparable from the dialogue and plot development. Both in dialogue and in visual actions, López Rubio has generally chosen the subtle allusion over the broad statement, and even in his historical plays he has avoided the excesses of pageantry and dramatic hyperbole by resorting to the simplest means of suggestion.

The playwright's most memorable characterizations have been women (Beatriz, Aunt Carolina, Gloria Velarde, Flora Vidal, Doña Rosa, and Inés de Castro—to name a few from various stages of his career), and his understanding of the female personality is a strong feature of many of his plays and television dramas. Women are frequently seen as victims or potential victims of the undependable male, or are exploited (like Leopoldina in *With Heart in Hand*); but they are endowed with wit, charm, intelligence, or other weapons of survival. In López Rubio's theater, love is continually presented as something that must be renewed to endure, and the process of renewal is achieved through the creation of illusion or theater—i.e., the dramatization of life itself.

The concern for illusion has caused many of his plays to be labeled "*teatro de evasión*." However, since this critical tag has been used to refer to works which vary considerably in theme and artistic value, especially by critics who are inimical to the poetical and fanciful in the theater, its validity is questionable. Clearly it is not applicable to a farcical comedy such as *Diana's Mind is Busy*, or to a somewhat melodramatic play like *Christmas Dinner*. And even when applied more appropriately to so subtle a work as *Alberto*, it must be qualified so that the psychological and poetic values of the play are not overlooked.

For such theorists of the contemporary Spanish theater as Alfonso Sastre and Juan Emilio Aragonés, López Rubio's plays do not meet their demands for a deeper involvement on the part of dramatists in a theater of social concern or agitation.[1] However, it cannot be said that the theater of López Rubio is not social in concept, despite its acknowledged boundaries. While his plays are invariably nonpolitical, moral or social concerns are in evidence in a number of them. In *Our Hands Are Innocent*, the dramatist considers the wider problem of human guilt and responsibility; *With Heart in Hand* deals with the special morality of business that permits manipulation and influence-peddling; and even the ironic, serious comedy *The Other Shore* is concerned with the moral ambivalence of contemporary man. In the teleplay *A Very Small Car*, the playwright deals ironically and satirically with the mindless acts of rebellion and violence among privileged young people.

López Rubio must be judged by what he has accomplished rather than for what he has not. Above all, he is a man of the theater whose wide experience has given him keen insight into the problems and needs of dramatic production. His plays have been created for a particular time and for a living stage, and he has sometimes avoided dramatic situations that might prove unacceptable or unpopular. In his most polished serious comedy, *The Blindfold*, he injects topical allusions and bits of colloquial speech to such an extent that many lines will lose their meaning in time; yet in spite of the topical humor, the strong human qualities lend the play an appeal that seems enduring. While López Rubio has also written with a constant awareness of the public for which his works are to be performed, he has insisted that the public participate in the theatrical experience, and throughout his career he has consciously striven to raise the taste of Spanish audiences.

Although López Rubio's plays have sometimes been compared with those of Miguel Mihura and Víctor Ruiz Iriarte, his work does not strongly resemble that of either writer. With Mihura he shares a common background and the literary associations of their youth and, on occasion, their sense of the comic, the absurd, or the ridiculous runs parallel. With Ruiz Iriarte there is a common Pirandellian affinity that is reflected in both dramatists' fondness for dramatic situations in which theater-within-theater develops. But whereas Ruiz Iriarte's characters tend more often to invent theater or dramatize a deceit for a specific goal, López Rubio's recognize their own theatricality from the start and play out life on their own stages. This application of Pirandellian techniques in his works recalls at times the more persistent Pirandellian bent of the French playwright Jean Anouilh; but the fascination for role-playing and the juxtaposition of illusion and reality are also part of a long Spanish tradition that stems from Cervantes and Calderón and that is continued in the twentieth century by Unamuno, Azorín, Casona, García Lorca, and a number of less renowned peninsular writers.

Whatever the influences on López Rubio's creative work, he has clearly established his own literary and dramatic identity. In 1952, he commented in his interview with Carlos Fernández Cuenca: "I have always had influences, but I don't believe I have ever been an imitator. I am professionally, as in my life, sincere." [2] It is a statement that is unlikely to be questioned.

Notes and References

Chapter One

1.   López Rubio's full baptismal name is "José Joaquín Julio Francisco Cesáreo Carraciolo Isaac de Santa Lucia y de la Santísima Trinidad." The certificate of baptism is reproduced in Antonio Gallego Morell's *Sesenta escritores granadinos con sus partidas de bautismo* (Granada, 1970).
2.   Described in an interview with Julián Cortés-Cavanillas, "Pepe López Rubio, el comediógrafo de espuma," *Los domingos de A B C* (Madrid, November 2, 1975), p. 22.
3.   Ibid., p. 23.
4.   Loosely: "Light at the tolling for the dead." Other references to this play will be by the original Spanish title.
5.   In the first scene of the play, Marcial visits his wife, Trinidad, after a separation of more than a year. He is informed that their daughter, María Paz, is engaged to a young Argentine, Luis Varela, who has seen the girl at the theater in Madrid and proposed by mail. At this point, Carlos Varela arrives, announcing that he is Luis's cousin and his "mano derecha" and that he has been sent to act as proxy in the wedding. María Paz falls in love with Carlos and is faced with the prospect of traveling to Argentina with him to meet Luis. The final act takes place on a transatlantic liner. When María Paz finally meets the man she supposes to be Luis, she admits that she loves Carlos. Then she discovers that the man she loves is in reality Carlos Luis Varela, her legal husband, and that she is talking to the real cousin, Luis Carlos Varela.
6.   Alejandro Miquis, "Semana teatral, *La Esfera*, XVI, No. 786 (January 26, 1929), pp. 6–7.
7.   For further information on the production of Spanish-language films in the early sound era and complete documentation of the contributions of López Rubio, Eduardo Ugarte, Jardiel Poncela, and others, see Alfonso Pinto's article "Hollywood's Spanish Language Films: A Neglected Chapter of the American Cinema, 1930–1935," *Films in Review*, XXIV, No. 8 (October 1973), pp. 474–81.
8.   Fernández Cuenca, "El autor y su obra preferida," *Correo literario*, No. 62 (December 15, 1952) p. 12.
9.   The actress Catalina Bárcena starred in all of the films based on works signed by G. Martínez Sierra. For information on the contribution of María Martínez Sierra to the works performed and/or published under her husband's name and the relationship of Martínez Sierra with Catalina Bárce-

na, see Patricia W. O'Connor's *Gregorio and María Martínez Sierra* (Boston, 1977).

10.   *Celos del aire* is a title that does not lend itself to a literal translation. The title chosen for my own English adaptation of this play is *In August We Play the Pyrenees.* For the sake of easy identification, the original Spanish title will be used in most references to this play except in the section devoted to a detailed analysis of the work.

11.   Alfredo Marquerie, *Veinte años de teatro en España* (Madrid, 1959), p. 108.

12.   Review reprinted in Sainz de Robles, *Teatro español, 1949–50*, p. 227.

13.   Eusebio García-Luengo, "Un año de teatro," *Indice*, VII, No. 47 (January 15, 1952), p. 13.

14.   Sainz de Robles, *Teatro español, 1951–52*, p. 12.

15.   Gonzalo Torrente Ballester, *Teatro español contemporáneo* (Madrid, 1957), p. 291.

16.   "La importancia de llamarse Ernesto," *Revista*, II, No. 63 (June 25–July 1, 1953), p. 14.

17.   "Un mes de teatro en Madrid," *Teatro*, No. 6 (April 1953), p. 6.

18.   *Teatro español contemporáneo*, pp. 293–94.

19.   "La venda en los ojos," *Teatro*, No. 10 (January-February-March 1954), p. 11.

20.   Enrique Sordo, "Escenarios Barceloneses," *Revista*, III, No. 130 (October 7–13, 1954), p. 10.

21.   "El teatro," *Destino*, XVIII, No. 896 (October 9, 1954), p. 33.

22.   Enrique Sordo, "Escenarios Barceloneses," *Revista*, IV, No. 157 (April 14–20, 1955), p. 14.

23.   Anthony M. Pasquariello and John V. Falconieri, Introduction to *La Otra Orilla* (New York, 1958), p. 12.

24.   Jardiel Poncela believed that Noel Coward had imitated his play. The ending of the Coward work does indeed bear a striking resemblance to the earlier Spanish comedy.

25.   In an article from *Triunfo*, reprinted in *Teatro español, 1958–59*, pp. 3–4.

26.   "Estreno de 'El corazón en la mano' de José López Rubio," *A B C*, edición semanal aérea (April 6, 1972), p. 11.

Chapter Two

1.   Other artists contributing illustrations to the book were Bartoluzzi, Barradas, Sancha, Tovar, Robledano, Bon, Pellicer, Areuger, Téllez, and Ramírez.

2.   Eugenio G. De Nora, *La novela española contemporánea (1927–1939)* (Madrid, 1969), p. 283.

3.   José López Rubio, *Roque Six* (Madrid, 1927), p. 239.

4. The judges for the *A B C* competition were the playwrights Eduardo Marquina, Carlos Arniches, and José Juan Cadenas.

5. Santorello, "Actualidad teatral," *Blanco y Negro*, XXXIX, No. 1967 (January 27, 1929), n.p.

6. Domingo Pérez Minik, *Debates sobre el teatro español contemporáneo* (Santa Cruz de Tenerife, 1953), pp. 222–23.

7. Gretchen Todd Starck, Introduction to *De la noche a la mañana* (New York, 1934), pp. xvii–xix.

8. "Semana teatral," *La Esfera*, XVI, No. 786 (January 26, 1929), p. 6.

9. All quotations of dialogue or stage directions from *De la noche a la mañana* and *La casa de naipes* are based on the Escelicer edition, Colección Teatro, No. 190 (Madrid, 1958).

10. The role of Silvia was created by Josefina Díaz, who became known to audiences in the United States much later in her career through her memorable performance as the mute grandmother in Carlos Saura's film *Cría cuervos*.

11. *La Esfera*, XVI, No. 786, p. 6.

12. Silvia's recommendation is the solution Beatriz adopts so ingeniously in López Rubio's later play *La venda en los ojos*.

13. *A B C*, No. 8554 (May 27, 1930), p. 45.

14. *A B C*, No. 8556 (May 29, 1930), p. 41.

15. "La semana teatral," *La Esfera*, XVII, No. 857 (June 7, 1930), p. 8 (photographs of the stage setting accompany this review of *La casa de naipes*).

16. A similar visual symbol is employed by Antonio Buero Vallejo at the end of the first act of *Historia de una escalera* (1949).

17. *A B C*, No. 8556, p. 41.

18. *La Esfera*, No. 857, p. 9.

Chapter Three

1. This and all subsequent quotations from *Alberto* are based on the Escelicer edition, Colección Teatro, No. 30 (Madrid, 1952).

2. Gonzalo Torrente Ballester, "Crónica de teatros," *Escorial*, XX (1949), pp. 420–21.

3. For a defense of the use of the fantastic in the literature of Spain, see remarks by Alejandro Casona in *Primer Acto*, No. 33 (April 1962), p. 2.

4. Lionel Abel, *Metatheatre* (New York, 1963), p. 79.

5. As has previously been noted in Chapter One, *Celos del aire* was performed in Italy under a quite different title.

6. Review from *A B C*, reprinted in Sainz de Robles, *Teatro español, 1949–50*, p. 224.

7. Review from *La Vanguardia*, reprinted in Sainz de Robles, *Teatro español, 1949–50*, p. 224.

8. Gonzalo Torrente Ballester, "Crónica de teatros," *Escorial*, XXI, No. 65 (January-February 1950), p. 224.

9.   Theodore S. Beardsley, Jr., "The Illogical Character in Contemporary Spanish Drama," *Hispania*, XLI (December 1958), p. 447.
10.   All references to and quotations from *Celos del aire are* based on the Escelicer edition, Colección Teatro, No. 2 (Madrid, 1951). The translations of dialogue are from my English adaptation.
11.   Marqueríe, *Veinte años de teatro en España*, p. 110.
12.   Enrique Vila Selma, "Correspondencia Guareschi-López Rubio," *Ateneo*, No. 86 (August 1, 1955), p. 6.
13.   Víctor Pradera, "Comentario teatral," *Arbor*, XV, No. 51 (March 1950), p. 440.

Chapter Four

1.   Reprinted in Sainz de Robles, *Teatro español, 1950–51*, pp. 301–302.
2.   All references to and quotations from *Veinte y cuarenta* are based on the Escelicer edition, Colección Teatro, No. 30 (Madrid, 1952).
3.   John Mason Brown, "What's Right with the Theatre," *Saturday Review* (May 11, 1963), p. 20.
4.   Torrente Ballester, *Teatro español contemporáneo*, p. 289.
5.   Prólogo to Sainz de Robles, *Teatro español, 1951–52*, p. 12.
6.   In Fernández Cuenca, "El autor y su obra preferida," p. 12.
7.   Julio Coll, "El teatro," *Destino*, XVI, No. 766 (April 12, 1952), p. 27.
8.   Examples would include O'Neill's *The Iceman Cometh*, Sherwood's *The Petrified Forest*, Inge's *Bus Stop*, Genet's *Le balcon*, and, more recently, Wilson's *The Hot l Baltimore*—as well as motion pictures such as *Ship of Fools, Stagecoach*, and most "disaster" films.
9.   All references to and quotations from *Cena de Navidad* are based on the Escelicer edition, Colección Teatro, No. 7 (Madrid, 1951).
10.   *Teatro español contemporáneo*, pp. 290–91.
11.   From the *autocrítica* reprinted in Sainz de Robles, *Teatro español, 1951–52*, p. 159.
12.   Ibid.
13.   Review from *España* reprinted in Sainz de Robles, *Teatro español, 1951–52*, p. 162.
14.   *Arbor*, XXI, No. 73 (January 1952), p. 119.
15.   *Veinte años de teatro en España*, p. 111.
16.   All references to and quotations from *Una madeja de lana azul celeste* are based on the Escelicer edition, Colección Teatro, No. 14 (Madrid, 1951).
17.   *Teatro español contemporáneo*, p. 291.
18.   *Veinte años de teatro en España*, p. 112.
19.   "Un comediógrafo español," *Insula*, No. 88 (April 15, 1953), p. 12.
20.   Ibid.
21.   Vásquez Zamora, "Un comediógrafo español," p. 12. The play was written for Tina Gascó and dedicated to her by the playwright. An opinion that differed from Vásquez Zamora's was given by Carlos Fernández Cuenca,

who praised the actress's performance in an article published in *Teatro*, No. 3 (January 1953).

22. Angel Valbuena Prat, *Historia del teatro español* (Barcelona, 1956), p. 672.

23. Reported by David Menor in "Teatro: el tema y la manera," *Ateneo*, No. 23 (December 6, 1952), p. 20.

24. José López Rubio, "El personaje," *Teatro*, No. 3 (January 1953), p. 35.

25. López Rubio describes Gerardo in this manner: "He is a playwright, slightly over fifty. He dresses with all the liberty that a correct man can allow himself in a place in the mountains, in summer and at midday, being a friend of the family and living close by. He has dispensed with the tie as the maximum concession, and has substituted a silk scarf " (Colección Teatro, No. 48, pp. 7–8). The dramatist might well be describing his own attire in the informal photograph appearing in Torrente Ballester's *Teatro español contemporáneo* (opposite p. 193). For a photograph of Carlos Casaravilla in the role of Gerardo, see *Teatro* (January 1953).

26. *Teatro español contemporáneo*, p. 292.

27. All references to and quotations from *El remedio en la memoria* are based on the Escelicer edition, Colección Teatro No. 48 (Madrid, 1952).

28. Carlos Fernández Cuenca, "Un mes de teatro en Madrid," *Teatro*, No. 3 (January 1953), p. 8.

29. *Metatheatre*, p. 59.

Chapter Five

1. Review by V. de la Serna y Répide, reprinted in Sainz de Robles, *Teatro español, 1953–54*, pp. 260–61.

2. *Teatro*, No. 10 (January-March 1954), p. 11.

3. Review from *Arriba*, reprinted in Sainz de Robles, *Teatro español, 1953–54*, p. 259.

4. "El teatro," *Revista*, No. 218 (June 14–20, 1956), p. 18.

5. Francisco Ruiz Ramón, *Historia del teatro español, Siglo XX* (Madrid, 1971), p. 354.

6. *Buero Vallejo, Sastre y el teatro de su tiempo* (New York, 1971), p. 34.

7. *The Blindfold* had its English-language premiere on August 23, 1977, at the Flat Rock Playhouse (North Carolina), where it was performed by the resident professional company.

8. *Teatro*, No. 3, p. 12.

9. All references to *La venda en los ojos* are based on the Escelicer edition, Colección Teatro, No. 101 (Madrid, 1954). Quotations of dialogue are from my translation in *The Modern Spanish Stage: Four Plays* (New York, 1970).

10. In the English translation, this humorous touch is necessarily lost.

11.   *The Idea of a Theater* (Princeton, 1949), p. 200.

12.   Expressed in the interview with Vásquez Zamora, "Un comediógrafo español," p. 12.

13.   For a consideration of Pirandello's influence in Ruiz Iriarte's plays, see Phyllis Zatlin Boring's "The Pirandellism of Víctor Ruiz Iriarte," *Estreno*, IV, 2 (1978), pp. 18–21.

14.   Review reprinted in Sainz de Robles, *Teatro español, 1954–55*, p. 261.

15.   "Los estrenos del Sábado de Gloria," *Revista*, IV, No. 157 (April 14–20, 1955), p. 19.

16.   *Veinte años de teatro en España*, pp. 112–13.

17.   In my English adaptation of *La otra orilla* (The Other Shore), the names of these characters have been changed to Pérez 138, Pérez 257, and Flora.

18.   *Veinte años de teatro en España*, pp. 113–14.

19.   All references to *La otra orilla* are based on the Escelicer edition, Colección Teatro, No. 119 (Madrid, 1955).

20.   A prime example of López Rubio's use of the telephone to create suspense or to startle the audience.

21.   In Jardiel Poncela's play, a dead husband returns as a ghost who interferes with his wife's second marriage and arranges her demise. In Coward's comedy, the dead wife returns with the intention of turning her husband into a ghost. Through a slip-up it is the second wife who is killed.

Chapter Six

1.   Enrique Sordo, "Escenarios Barceloneses," *Revista*, III, No. 130 (October 7–13, 1954), p. 10.

2.   Julio Coll, "El teatro," *Destino*, No. 896 (October 9, 1954), p. 33.

3.   All references to *Cuenta nueva* are based on a manuscript copy of the play which was provided by José López Rubio.

4.   Mercedes's complaint about censorship is not really exaggerated. Such changes through dubbing were actually made in Spain at the time the play was written—at times with amusing results that were missed by the censors.

5.   A few years later, López Rubio would base his comedy *Diana está comunicando* on the concept of thought and personality transferal.

6.   "El teatro: *La novia del espacio*," *Revista*, V, No. 202 (February 23–29, 1956), p. 20. Sordo's comments are quoted at length since they provide the most detailed information available on the shortlived play.

7.   The ending of *La novia del espacio* shows a distinct resemblance to the climax of the film *Close Encounters of the Third Kind* (1977), in which the visual effect of the returning spaceship is complemented by musical effects.

Obviously, special effects of this sort are easier to achieve on film than in live performance.

8.   In a letter to the author dated December 20, 1962, the playwright wrote: "I have always thought of revising this work, whose theme commands new interest from time to time. It is the [theme] of flying saucers, and its action is developed in 'a place in La Mancha.' With the dramatic situation removed and the action carried more toward the absurd, with the difficult 'flying saucer–poetry' formula put aside, I believe that it can prove viable." However, López Rubio's interest in the work has never been rekindled sufficiently for him to revise the play.

9.   *Veinte años de teatro en España*, p. 114.

10.   "Teatro en Madrid: Los famosos en cartel," *Revista*, V, No. 234 (October 4–10, 1956), p. 19.

11.   "El teatro," *Revista*, VI, No. 287 (October 12–18, 1957), p. 10.

12.   All references to and quotations from *Un trono para Cristy* are based on the Escelicer edition, Colección Teatro, No. 174 (Madrid, 1957).

13.   *Autocrítica* reprinted in Sainz de Robles, *Teatro español, 1958–59*, p. 3.

14.   Review from *Ya* by N. González Ruiz, reprinted in Sainz de Robles, *Teatro español, 1958–59*, p. 8.

15.   "Las manos son inocentes," *Indice*, XII, No. 119 (November 1958), p. 19.

16.   Review from *España*, reprinted in Sainz de Robles, *Teatro español, 1958–59*, p. 5.

17.   "Prologo" to *Teatro español, 1958–59*, pp. xviii–xix.

18.   "El teatro," *Revista*, VIII, No. 388 (September 19, 1959) p. 22.

19.   *Veinte años de teatro en España*, p. 116.

20.   "Luces de candilejas," *La Hora*, No. 96 (October 30, 1958), p. 23.

21.   All references to and quotations from *Las manos son inocentes* are based on the Escelicer edition, Coleccion Teatro, No. 272 (Madrid, 1960).

22.   The reversal of a situation in tragedy is described by Aristotle: "Reversal of the Situation is a change by which the action veers round to its opposite, subject always to our rule of probability or necessity. Thus in *Oedipus*, the messenger comes to cheer Oedipus and free him from his alarms about his mother, but by revealing who he is produces the opposite effect. . . . Recognition, as the name indicates, is a change from ignorance to knowledge, producing love or hate between persons destined by the poet for good or bad fortune. The best form of recognition is coincident with a Reversal of a Situation. . . . There are indeed other forms. Even inanimate things of the most trivial kind may in a sense be objects of recognition. Again, we may recognize whether a person has done a thing or not." *Poetics*, trans. S. S. Butcher (New York, 1961), pp. 72–73.

23.   José Castellano, "Teatro," *La estafeta literaria*, No. 150 (October 18, 1958), p. 10.

Chapter Seven

1. "Prólogo" to *Teatro español, 1959–60*, p. xvi.
2. All references to and quotations from *Diana está counicado* are based on the Escelicer edition, Colcección Teatro, No. 331 (Madrid, 1962).
3. "Teatro professional," *Primer Acto*, Nos. 29–30 (December 1961–January 1962), pp. 68–69.
4. In his complete *autocrítica*, reprinted in *Teatro español, 1961–62*, p. 3, López Rubio recalled that critics had not noticed that he was satirizing the frivolous society of *Un trono para Cristy* some years earlier, and he emphasized that the world depicted in *Esta noche, tampoco* did exist—although he did not defend it or necessarily admire it. He also noted that the play had been designed for Conchita Montes and that a playwright should take care not to write a rural tragedy for the acclaimed comedienne.
5. Reprinted in Sainz de Robles, *Teatro español, 1964–65*, p. 195.
6. In a review from *Arriba*, reprinted in Sainz de Robles, *Teatro español, 1964–65*, pp. 197–99.
7. In a review from *Pueblo*, reprinted in *Teatro español, 1964–65*, pp. 198–99.
8. All references to and quotations from *Nunca es tarde* are based on the Escelicer edition, Colección Teatro, No. 464 (Madrid, 1965).
9. Each act of *Nunca es tarde* is set in a different location, and consequently the play was relatively expensive to stage. The *prólogo* and *intermedio*, which were omitted in the Madrid production, were intended to be performed with amplified voices before a simple drop curtain, which would not have added appreciably to the cost of production.
10. The role of the architect was performed by the same actor (Enrique Diosdado) who portrayed Miguel in the first and second acts.
11. Review reprinted in Sainz de Robles, *Teatro español, 1964–65*, p. 198.
12. This is the playwright's own label for *Las manos son inocentes*. He calls *La puerta del ángel* simply a "drama en dos actos."
13. The analysis of *La puerta del ángel* and quotations from this play are based on the manuscript which the playwright permitted me to read in June 1971 and again in October 1977.
14. This passage also explains the title of the play.
15. The new ending was described by the playwright in a personal conversation with him in October 1977.
16. For further comments on *Veneno activo*, see Chapter Eight.
17. "Estreno de 'El corazón en la mano' de López Rubio," *A B C*, edición semanal aérea (April 6, 1972), p. 11.
18. All references to and quotations from *El corazón de la mano* are based on the Escelicer edition, Colección Teatro, No. 759 (Madrid, 1974).
19. There are certain reminscences of Mateo–Don Mateo from López Rubio's *De la noche a la mañana* in Eduardo's pursuit of Mapy. However,

Silvia, the object of interest in López Rubio's first play, is utterly theatrical in concept and charmingly clever in her special, illogical world. Mapy, on the other hand, is far more realistically drawn; and Eduardo is irrationally attracted to her in spite of her lack of imagination, wit, or intellect.

Chapter Eight

1. Published by Ediciones Guadarrama (Madrid, 1971).

2. Although the playwright describes the episode entitled *La parroca* as "an Iberian fantasy," the only thing fantastic about it is the idea of the marriage (and possible divorce) of a priest. The actual treatment is quite realistic, and the results of the marriage are highly probable. In a few episodes there is a suggestion of the supernatural.

3. Mingote, a contemporary of López Rubio, is Spain's most illustrious cartoonist. The two characters in *Antes y después* would be easily recognizable to Spanish audiences.

4. That a play (even a comic one) in which marriage and divorce for a priest were portrayed could be presented on Spanish television is indicative of the degree of censorial relaxation (at least on some subjects) that had occurred in Spain by 1969.

5. Café-theater was at its peak of popularity at the time of the staging of *Veneno activo*. The few café-theaters that remained in Madrid in 1978 were cabarets that present satirical or erotic musicals or skits on a small scale.

6. "*Veneno* y sopas de ajo" (October 23, 1971), p. 8.

7. The Spanish "su" is a third-person possessive adjective that means "his, her, their." Given the development of the dramatic action, the words could possibly have any of these meanings; but at the end of the play, "his" or "her" great love is, at least momentarily, "their" great love.

8. In *La otra orilla* and *Las manos son inocentes*, the phone calls are used for suspense and revelation. In *Esta noche, tampoco*, there are telephone "monologues," a bit like those of *La venda en los ojos*. The telephone call in *Nunca es tarde* conveys a tragic message to a character and creates a feeling of dread in the audience. In *El corazón en la mano*, a character is introduced indirectly by phone. In the teleplay *Igual, igual*, a tape recorder is employed with a special dramatic function.

9. The other plays in the series are: *Las limosnas* (The Alms), dealing ironically with honesty and trust; *El de la suerte* (The Lucky Ticket), which is the story of a man who throws away a winning lottery ticket to avoid the greed of his family and friends that he has foreseen in a dream. This episode uses visual effects extensively and is unique in that it permits the viewer to look directly into the thoughts of a character; *Un cochecito pequeño* (A Very Small Car), which treats ironically the thoughtless rebellion and vandalism of young rich teenagers; *El cielo abierto* (Heaven with Open Arms), dealing with a young nun who may or may not be insane. She succeeds in convincing the passengers in a train compartment that they are on their way to heaven; and

Igual, igual (Exactly the Same), which centers on a man who writes his wife to tell her that life continues "exactly the same" while she is away on vacation. Ironically, he continues to deceive her exactly the same way as when she is at home. An unusual touch in this episode is the tape recording of the wife's voice that the husband plays at a speed that turns the words into gibberish.

10.   Described in Pilar Trenas's interview "José López Rubio y sus 'Mujeres insólitas,' " *Los domingos de A B C* (October 3, 1976), p. 52.

11.   In the Trenas interview, López Rubio uses the English word "hobby" to describe his interest in history. It is, of course, a hobby to which he has dedicated himself with the thoroughness of a specialist.

12.   Trenas, "José López Rubio y sus 'Mujeres insólitas,' " p. 53.

13.   We may assume that the selection of the name "Pepe" for the stage manager, who is present in each play, was not coincidental.

14.   In a personal letter from José López Rubio dated June 26, 1978.

15.   The titles of the fourteen episodes and the subject of each are given in the bibliography.

16.   Trenas, "José López Rubio . . . ," p. 53.

17.   Paso's *Preguntan por Julio César* (1960) turns Cleopatra into a caricature. The play is not memorable.

18.   From the unpublished manuscript of *La dama de las camelias*, p. 44.

19.   *Ibid.*, pp. 44–45.

20.   Even the most casual comparison of López Rubio's plays with the stage works of the writers mentioned will confirm his very personal and original approach to history.

Chapter Nine

1.   For a detailed presentation of Sastre's theories of drama, see: *Drama y sociedad* (Madrid, 1956). Juan Emilio Aragonés's ideas on the purpose of theater and his criticism of the Spanish theater can be found in the following articles: "Tres caminos del teatro," *Revista*, II, No. 86 (December 3–9, 1953), p. 14; "Tres caminos del teatro: Teatro comprometido," *Revista*, II, No. 90 (December 31, 1953–January 6, 1954), p. 14; and "Tres caminos del teatro: Teatro testimonial," *Revista*, III, No. 91 (January 7–13, 1954), p. 14.

2.   "El autor y su obra preferida," p. 10.

Selected Bibliography

PRIMARY SOURCES

1. In English

The Blindfold. Trans. Marion Holt. In *The Modern Spanish Stage: Four Plays.* Ed. Marion Holt. New York: Hill & Wang, 1970. (The only play by López Rubio published in English to date.)

2. In Spanish

The following plays of López Rubio have been published by Escelicer in the "Colección Teatro" (CT). Not all are currently in print.

Celos del aire (CT 2), *Cena de Navidad* (CT 7), *Una madeja de lana azul celeste* (CT 14), *Alberto* and *Veinte y cuarenta* (CT 30), *El remedio en la memoria* (CT 48), *Estoy pensado en ti* (one act, included in CT 100), *La venda en los ojos* (CT 101), *La otra orilla* (CT 119), *El caballero de Barajas* (CT 151), *Un trono para Cristy* (CT 174), *De la noche a la mañana* and *La casa de naipes* (CT 190), *Las manos son inocentes* (CT 272), *Diana está comunicando* (CT 331), *Esta noche, tampoco* (CT 461), *Nunca es tarde* (CT 464), *El corazón en la mano* (CT 759).

The following translations and adaptations by López Rubio have also appeared in the "Colección Teatro" (CT), but only a few remain in print.

Tovarich (Deval) (CT 4), *La muerte de un viajante* (Miller) (CT 12), *La plaza de Berkeley* (Balderston) (CT 23), *La esposa constante* (Maugham) (CT 26), *La importancia de llamarse Ernesto* (Wilde) (CT 39), *Sombra querida* (Deval) (CT 82), *Crimen perfecto* (Knott) (CT 138), *El avaro* (Molière) (CT 263), *Un domingo en Nueva York* (Krasna) (CT 466), *La Baiiiiia* (Adrien) (CT 599).

The following plays by López Rubio have been included in the yearly anthology *Teatro español,* published by Aguilar and edited by F. Sainz de Robles, with selected reviews and the author's *autocríticas.*

Celos del aire (1949–50), *Veinte y cuarenta* (1950–51), *Una madeja de lana azul celeste* (1951–52), *La venda en los ojos* (1953–54), *La otra orilla* (1954–55), *Las manos son inocentes* (1958–59), *Diana está comunicando* (1959–60), *Esta noche, tampoco* (1961–62), *Nunca es tarde* (1964–65).

Other editions of dramatic works:

Teatro selecto de José López Rubio. Madrid: Escelicer, 1969. With prologue by Alfredo Marqueríe. Contains *Celos del aire, La venda en los ojos, La otra orilla, Las manos son inocentes, Nunca es tarde.*

Al filo de lo imposible. Madrid: Ediciones Guadarrama, 1971. With introduc-

tion by José Luis Herrera. Contains the scripts of the sixteen episodes of López Rubio's first series for television.
For the preparation of this study, the following unpublished dramatic works by López Rubio were consulted in manuscript form:
Cuenta nueva (comedia en tres actos).
La puerta del ángel (drama en dos actos).
Mujeres insólitas: La segunda señora Tudor (Anne Boleyn), *Nuestra señora de Termidor* (Teresa Cabarrús), *La sierpe del Nilo* (Cleopatra), *El ángel atostigador* (la Marquesa de Brinvilliers), *La monja Alférez* (Catalina de Erauso), *Lola Montes* (María Dolores Elisa Gilbert), *El collar de la reina* (Madame de La Motte), *La bruja de Venecia* (Blanca Capello), *La reina loca* (Juana de Castilla), *La mujer sin nombre* (La Marquesa de Douhault), *La reina después de muerta* (Inés de Castro), *La dama de las camelias* (Alfonsina Plessis), *La tumultuosa Princesa de Eboli* (Doña Ana de Mendoza), *La viuda roja* (Margarita Steinheil).

3. Nondramatic Works by López Rubio
Cuentos inverosímiles. Madrid: Rafael Caro Raggio, 1924.
Roque Six. Madrid: R. Caro Raggio, 1927.

4. Articles by López Rubio
"El personaje," *Teatro*, No. 3 (January 1953), 35–36.
"Encuentro con Charlie," *Los domingos de A B C* (January 8, 1978), 14–15.

SECONDARY SOURCES

1. In English
BEARDSLEY, THEODORE S., JR. "The Illogical Character in Contemporary Spanish Drama," *Hispania*, XLI (December 1958), 445–49. An article which touches on López Rubio's play *Celos del aire*.
HOLCOMB, GEORGE LAWRENCE. *The Theatre in Spain since 1939.* Doctoral dissertation, University of Texas, 1959. A useful source for information on the Spanish theater of the period immediately following the Civil War. It contains résumés of many plays.
HOLT, MARION P. "López Rubio's Venture into Serious Drama," *Hispania*, XLIX, 4 (December 1966), 764–68. An analysis of *Las manos son inocentes* that is slightly more detailed than the one provided in the present study.
————. "López Rubio's *Alberto*: Character Revelation and Form," *Modern Drama*, 10, 2 (September 1967), 144–50. A detailed analysis of the play that initiated López Rubio's second career as a dramatist in 1949.
————. *The Contemporary Spanish Theater (1949–1972).* Boston: Twayne, 1975. The only comprehensive study of the post–Civil War Spanish theater that is available in English. Pages 34–51 deal specifically with López Rubio.

PASQUARIELLO, ANTHONY M., and FALCONIERI, JOHN V. Introduction to *La otra orilla*. New York: Appleton-Century-Crofts, 1958. A brief presentation of López Rubio's career to 1958 and a consideration of the major plays he had written.

PINTO, ALFONSO. "Hollywood's Spanish-language Films: A Neglected Chapter of the American Cinema, 1930–1935," *Films in Review*, XXIV, 8 (October 1973), 474–83. This article documents the work done by López Rubio, Ugarte, Jardiel Poncela and others at MGM and Fox studios. Highly recommended for information on the period of Spanish-language film production in the United States.

STARCK, GRETCHEN TODD. Introduction to *De la noche a la mañana*. New York: W. W. Norton and Co., 1934. A detailed analysis of López Rubio's first work to appear in textbook form.

WADE, GERALD E. Introduction to *Un trono para Cristy*. New York: Dodd, Mead and Co., 1960. A brief description of López Rubio's position in the Spanish theater in 1959, with emphasis on the lighter aspects of his work.

WARREN, VIRGIL ALEXANDER, and CAVAZOS, NELSON AUGUSTO. Introduction to *Una madeja de lana azul celeste*. Englewood Cliffs, N.J.: Prentice-Hall, 1969. Provides general information on the playwright but no critical analysis of the work in question.

2. In Spanish

ALBERTI, SANTIAGO. "El hombre y su idea: José López Rubio," *Revista*, II, 59 (May 28–June 3, 1953), 11. An interview with López Rubio at the time he was writing *Cuenta nueva*, touching on his work as a translator.

CARBALLO, J. ROF., et al. *El teatro de humor en España*. Madrid: Editora Nacional, 1966. Essays by various authors on the nature of humor in the modern Spanish theater. Not all are of equal interest. Pages 155–68 deal specifically with the work of López Rubio.

CORTÉS, ELADIO. "Charla con José López Rubio," *Estreno*, IV, 2 (1978), 6–11. An extensive and frank interview with López Rubio conducted by Cortés in January 1976 but published after the completion of the present book. Recommended.

CORTES-CAVANILLAS, JULIÁN. "Pepe López Rubio, el comediógrafo de espuma," *Los domingos de A B C* (November 2, 1975), 22–24. The frankest and most comprehensive interview that López Rubio has given on his private and professional life. Recommended.

DOWLING, JOHN. "Teatro cómico y lo cómico en el teatro español de la posguera,"*Hispania*, 60, 4 (December 1977), 899–906. An interesting article explaining the special nature of Spanish comedy and the types of theater considered comic in the post–Civil War period. The article does not, however, deal in any specific way with the plays of López Rubio.

FERNÁNDEZ CUENCA, CARLOS. "El autor y su obra preferida," *Correo literario*, III, 62 (December 15, 1952), 10–12. A long interview conducted with López Rubio shortly after the premiere of *El remedio en la memoria*. It provides valuable insight into the playwright's approach to theater and his writing habits.

FLÓREZ, RAFAEL. *Mío Jardiel*. Madrid: Biblioteca Nueva, 1966. Although the author's style can be annoying, this biography is recommended because of the record it provides of Jardiel's associations with López Rubio both in the Madrid of the 1920s and during the Hollywood years.

GÓMEZ-SANTOS, MARINO. "Como vive José López Rubio," *Ya*, June 24, 1977, p. 23. This recently published interview with López Rubio offers a few details on the playwright's life that were not disclosed in earlier interviews.

HOLT, MARION P. Introduction to *La venda en los ojos*. New York: Appleton-Century-Crofts, 1966. A concise analysis of López Rubio's dramatic techniques and of one of his best plays.

MARQUERÍE, ALFREDO. *Veinte años de teatro en España*. Madrid: Editora Nacional, 1959. Recommended for the critiques of López Rubio's earlier plays by the late critic. Pages 105–16 deal specifically with López Rubio.

MIQUIS, ALEJANDRO. "Semana teatral," *La Esfera*, XVI, 786, January 26, 1929, pp. 6–7. A detailed and perceptive review of López Rubio's first play with Ugarte.

————. "La casa de naipes," *La Esfera*, XVII, 857, June 7, 1930, n.p. A review of López Rubio's second play with Ugarte, including photographs of the cast and set.

NORA, EUGENIO G. DE. *La novela española contemporánea (1927–1939)*. Madrid: Editorial Gredos, 1968, 281–83. An appreciative analysis of López Rubio's single novel by a leading Spanish authority.

RODRÍGUEZ, MIGUEL LUIS. "El ingenioso teatro de José López Rubio," *Indice*, XII, 122 (February 1959), 18. A commentary on López Rubio's earlier plays that includes both praise and negative criticism.

RODRÍGUEZ ALCALDE, LEOPOLDO. *Teatro español contemporáneo*. Madrid: Epesa, 1973, 169–72. A survey of twentieth-century peninsular theater, its writers, actors, and directors. The section on López Rubio is brief and superficial.

RUIZ RAMÓN, FRANCISCO. *Historia del teatro español, 2: Siglo veinte*. Madrid: Alianza Editorial, 1971, 353–55. The most comprehensive work in Spanish on the modern theater of Spain. Although the author does not deal extensively with López Rubio's plays, he gives respectful attention to *La venda en los ojos*.

SANZ DE SOTO, EMILIO. "Los recuerdos de 'La traviesa molinera,'"*Triunfo*, XXIX, 632, November 9, 1974, pp. 62–65. An article on the "lost" film *La traviesa molinera* and an interview with Hilda Moreno, who starred in the Spanish, English, and French versions. She recalls López Rubio's script for *El último varón sobre la tierra* and her work in that film. Her interesting reminiscences shed further light on the degree to which Spanish artists and writers were involved in film-making in the 1930s.

TORRENTE BALLESTER, GONZALO. *Teatro español contemporáneo.* Madrid: Ediciones Guadarrama, 1957. Contains concise reviews of five of López Rubio's plays on pages 288–300.

TRENAS, PILAR. "José López Rubio y sus 'Mujeres insólitas,' " *Los domingos de A B C*, October 3, 1976, pp. 52–53. Interesting details on the writing and production of López Rubio's second television series.

VALBUENA PRAT, ANGEL. *Historia del teatro español.* Barcelona: Noguer, 1956, 671–73. Contains analyses of *Celos del aire* and *El remedio en la memoria.*

VÁZQUEZ ZAMORA, RAFAEL. "Un comediógrafo español: López Rubio," *Insula,* VIII, 88 (April 15, 1953), 12. An interview in which the playwright gives his reactions to the criticism and performance of *El remedio en la memoria* and expresses opinions and thoughts on Pirandello, Moratín, O'Neill, and other dramatists. Recommended.

ZÚÑIGA, ANGEL. *Una historia del cine* (2 vols.). Barcelona: Ediciones Destino, 1948, Vol. 1, 391, Vol 2, 361–65. Comments on López Rubio's contributions to Spanish motion pictures prior to 1948.

3.   In French

SOLSONA, BRAULIO. "Le Théâtre en Espagne," *La Revue Theatrale*, 8, 24 (1953), 28–32. Evaluation of the Spanish theater of the early 1950s, with favorable comments on the plays of López Rubio.

Index